The Blind
Girl's Song

The Blind Girl's Song

Fanny Crosby

Lucille Travis

CF4•K

10 9 8 7 6 5 4 3
Copyright © 2013 Lucille Travis
Reprinted in 2015 and 2016

paperback ISBN 978-1-78191-163-1
epub ISBN 978-1-78191-214-0
mobi ISBN 978-1-78191-215-7

Published by
Christian Focus Publications,
Geanies House, Fearn, Tain, Ross-shire,
IV20 1TW, Scotland, U.K.
Tel: 01862 871011
Fax: 01862 871699

www.christianfocus.com
email: info@christianfocus.com

Cover design by Daniel van Straaten
Cover illustration by Brent Donahoe
American English is used throughout this book
Printed and bound in Denmark
by Nørhaven

Contents

To Christine:
From the beginning you were a precious gift from God, dear daughter!
This book is for you, with the prayer that no matter how dark the night around may be, your heart will sing in the light of Jesus all your days.

Through Grandmother's Eyes

Above the low hills of Putnam County, New York the faint light of dawn touched the trees and scattered farmhouses of Southeast's mostly poor farms. After the hard cold winter of 1820, April's first flowers were beginning to show. In one small farmhouse surrounded by fields and a low stone wall, lights shone from the windows. They had been on all night.

Behind a half-curtained window, a mother sat in a rocking chair holding her small infant in her arms. At last the baby's cries had stopped and she slept. The mother's head bent low over her child, her eyes closed and the rocking chair was still.

At the door, Grandmother Eunice stood for a moment, giving thanks in her heart that at last the terrible night was over. Taking care not to wake either her daughter, Mercy, or the baby, she gently lifted her tiny grandchild, Frances, from Mercy's arms and placed her in the cradle next to the rocker. Satisfied both mother and child were fast asleep, she tiptoed from the room.

In the kitchen her younger daughter, Theda, was already filling plates for three-year-old Polly and young Joseph who was nearly as tall as his father, Sylvanus.

Eunice took her seat as Joseph looked up. "Pa and John went down to the barn," he pointed out. "Pa said not to wait for them. I can take breakfast down to them as soon as I'm done."

Eunice nodded. "It's been a long night for all of us, and I'm guessing John couldn't stand to hear his first born child suffering another minute. You be sure and tell him his wife and baby are both asleep now."

Theda slapped her wooden serving spoon down hard on the table and sat down. "Doctor or no doctor, whoever that man was who came last night, I can't believe putting those hot poultices on a six-week-old infant's eyes won't do more harm than good. I never heard such pitiful cries coming out of that poor little thing." Theda wiped away the tears that filled her own eyes.

"Now, daughter," Eunice said, "your father went all the way to Doansburg for the doctor, and if he'd been there he would have come. Be glad that man, stranger or not, was a doctor and offered his help. I'll admit using hot poultices didn't set well with me either, but it was clear the infection was bad and something had to be done. Let's give thanks and trust in God's good will."

By the end of a week the infection did seem to be better, but thick white scars had covered the eyes, and soon Eunice knew that her six-week-old grandchild could no longer see. Sadness settled like a cloud over the household. But Grandmother Eunice was a woman of strong faith. "Now daughter," she reminded Mercy, "what can't be cured, can be endured." It was an old Puritan saying, and the Crosby family knew it well. Their family line went straight back to the Puritans who had first come to America on the Mayflower. Eunice and her family were poor, but they were hard workers with the same faith and courage as their Puritan ancestors. Before the year was out Mercy's husband, John, died suddenly, and baby Fanny as he had fondly called her, was fatherless. Her mother was soon working as a maid to help support the family.

"God will provide," Grandmother Eunice sang as she rocked and cared for her grandchild. She had already decided that little Fanny would learn to do the same things as sighted children. "And why not?" she said. "All babies come into this world ready to learn, don't they?" she said, tickling Fanny's small chin. "Didn't I come from a family of eleven, and your grandpa, one of nineteen children?" Her tickling was making Fanny laugh. "That's right, little one, you're laughing just like any baby does when its Grandma tickles it. You will do well, Fanny Crosby!"

Fanny grew up to know every path and field near the farmhouse and every room with its furniture inside the house. Her grandmother had taught her well, and Fanny picked up sounds and smells and the touch of things quickly. From a toddler she'd learned directions and remembered them as she did everything she learned. At three years of age she had thought it was grandmother who needed to hold her hand. Today the October sun felt warm on her face and the ground under her bare feet drier and harder than summer earth.

"Fanny, I should have made you put on your shoes, child. We will have to watch out for the prickly burrs that love to ride whatever comes by." Fanny knew by the flap-flap of grandmother's steps that she was wearing her old gardening shoes.

"You know, Grandma, that my feet love to feel as much as the rest of me," Fanny said. Grandma answered with a little squeeze of her hand and a soft chuckle. "Oh listen, Grandma," Fanny said as she stood still. She turned her head slightly. "Hear it?" she asked. "It's a bird calling in the tree near us for I can hear it moving on one of the branches. But it's not one of the ones we know."

"That, child, is a whippoorwill, and you can hear him calling his name. And I see him, Fanny, just where you are pointing, over in a maple tree on one of the low branches." For a moment they stood and listened until the bird called again. "Now, let me tell you what he looks like, Fanny. If you add its nice white bristled tail, he's not much bigger than the small oat loaves we sometimes make together. Its wings are mottled, brown and gray and black, and its breast is reddish brown."

Once Fanny had seen the faintest glimmer of shining colors in a sunset when she and Grandmother stood at the top of a high hill. Grandmother had taught her the names of the colors. She could tell when it was day from the faint brightness that Grandma said was like looking through a window frosted over with winter ice so thick that nothing else could be seen. She knew too when night came and the faint light was gone. Happily she could see all she needed with her ears and hands and feet and nose, and imagine all that anyone described for her.

Fanny heard her grandmother step to the side of the path and then the rustling of dry weeds and the sounds grandmother always made when she pulled weeds in the garden. In a moment she was back. "Here child, I believe I've mixed these well enough to give you the feel of bristled." Fanny reached to touch the small bundle her grandmother held, and let her fingers run over the mix.

"I see it," she cried, and she did see it with her hands, at once knowing what the word bristled meant. "What a fine new bird to add to our list." Fanny heard her grandmother throw away the bundled weeds, brush her hands on her skirts, but she didn't take Fanny's hand yet.

"Now, child, tell me just who is on our list and how many we know so far."

Quickly, Fanny named them one by one: the red-headed woodpecker, the mockingbird with its white chin, and the bird with a garment of blue, and the red-winged blackbird.

"Good, child," her grandmother said, "and soon we will learn about the meadowlark, the cuckoo, the yellow warbler, the wren, the songsparrow, the goldfinch, and the robin, but today how would you like to play a special game?"

"Yes, yes, Grandma, please let's, but I can hardly wait to learn all the birds. God has made so many."

"He has, Fanny, and you and I whenever we take our walks together are walking inside God's great book just full of the things he has made for us to learn from and enjoy. Do you remember what the Bible says about us and the little common birds?"

Fanny squeezed her grandmother's fingers. In the mornings Grandma taught her the Bible, line after line, chapter after chapter. Everything she heard and repeated she stored in her memory. It was like there were shelves in her mind neatly stored with each thing she learned, all ready and waiting to be called whenever she needed them. "Yes," she said, "Jesus told us that even with so many birds to care for, the heavenly Father has no trouble feeding them, and he said we are more valuable than those birds, and he easily cares for us," she recited in her own words. "I can hear you smiling, Grandma."

"I was smiling at your way of putting God's promise to us, but how did you know?"

"When you smile, Grandma, sometimes I can hear the little move you make with your mouth, the tiny click of teeth. I know your face so well I know the direction your mouth is going, up not down."

"Well," her grandmother said, "you also know whether I have reason to be stern or happy."

"Yes, but I can tell lots of things, like you are wearing your everyday long black dress because you've rolled back those stiff cuffs. And I can feel the buttons down the front are worn and not the nice new ones on your good Sunday dress."

"And don't I know that your mother has told you that all Southeast women wear long black dresses with stiff white cuffs and buttons down to the waist, and save the best for Sunday," Grandma said and chuckled.

"Ah, this is the spot I've been looking for, Fanny, for our game. Come sit here on this old log right next to me." In a moment Fanny was seated on the log. "Now, child," her grandmother began, "all around us are trees, maple, oak, a wild apple tree, birch, even an ancient cherry tree. Do you remember yesterday's wind how it whistled around the house? Well, it has made a lovely mix of leaves off the trees here, and blown some of them up against our log. You know the trees by touching their bark and feeling the shape of their leaves, even smelling them and tracing the veins on their leaves, so here is our game for today. Shall we see if you can tell which of these leaves belonged to which tree? Remember the leaves are drier now and some are curled, even a bit broken, but you may feel until you find the best of the lot."

Eagerly Fanny knelt by the log feeling for the piles of leaves and carefully sorting among them. Sometimes she held them to her nose, some she quickly put aside and others she piled into her skirt. When she was satisfied with her pile she held them up one by one and gave the name of their tree, then set them aside. Only once did she hesitate over a shriveled cherry leaf, smelled it again, felt it, and firmly said, "cherry tree." She had identified perfectly all of the leaves in her pile, and again heard her grandma smile. The day ended all too soon.

Fanny liked evening meal time when Grandpa and uncle Joseph came in from the fields, Mother came home from work, and Aunt Theda and Grandmother called them all to supper. The little house filled up quickly. She and Polly who was almost three years older than herself, though Polly was her aunt too, were always the last to sit down at the table. Fanny giggled, thinking as she slid onto the bench next to Polly, that they were also the first to leave to join the village children playing outdoors. When it grew dark and mothers called their children home, Fanny, who could not see with her eyes and played just as well in the dark was the last to leave. She easily climbed trees, played the games the others played, even rode bareback when she had a mind to. Of Grandpa's two horses, old Dobbin knew her, and let her hold on tight to his mane while she urged him to run. It drove Luke, who worked in the barn, wild though she tried to tell him that Dobbin would never run into anything. Her mother would have protected her from many things, but Grandmother knew Fanny could and would do most anything sighted children did, including getting into mischief.

Evenings before bedtime were never dull in Fanny's family. Grandpa and her mother took turns reading aloud exciting stories and poems. Fanny's favorites were tales of robbers, stories of the Wild West, of Greek heroes, and John Bunyan's *Pilgrim's Progress*.

Later upstairs in her bed if she listened carefully she could hear Grandpa reading aloud tales of the strange knight Don Quixote, or the robber chieftain Rinaldo Rhinaldine. "I shall be a soldier when I am grown," Fanny would tell herself, "or maybe a sailor and have adventures." Sundays when they walked barefoot to church, carrying their shoes until they came to the church, she thought she might become a minister. She was sure she could preach a better sermon than the pastor.

When she sat on the hard bench in the little church it seemed to Fanny that the preacher's sermons would never end. Week after week, Fanny could hear the heavy breathing and light snore now and then of the men who were dozing into their long beards. Others smoked clay pipes and filled the air with the smell of tobacco. She was happy when the congregation got to sing. Since the church was too poor for books, one of the deacons would always do what was called lining out the Psalm. The deacon would sing one line of a Psalm, and the congregation would repeat it until they had finished the Psalm. Fanny loved to sing and could have gone on much longer.

Fanny knew one place where Bible stories came alive, and where prayer was really talking to God. It was at her grandmother's rocking chair. Grandma made the Bible stories real and explained them so that she and Polly could understand. It was a kind Heavenly Father who sent his only son, Jesus Christ into the world to save it and be a Friend to all mankind. We could ask him for everything. "But," she would add, "remember that if God does not give you what you ask, then he has something better in store for you." Fanny would not forget. Her mother wanted more than anything for Fanny's eyes to be healed.

"Soon, Fanny will go and visit a doctor who knows all about eyes and see how he can help us." Fanny listened but thought little more about it, until the day her mother packed their things and said, "We leave tomorrow morning."

Fanny wanted her grandmother to come with them on the trip to New York City, but mother said no. "It will take all the money I've saved since you were born," her mother said, "for the two of us to go and see Dr Mott at his eye clinic in New York. But just think how wonderful it will be if he can fix your eyes, child."

First she and her mother had ridden in the wagon all the way to the town of Sing Sing. By the time they went on board the boat waiting to take them on the Hudson River for the rest of the trip to New York, Fanny wanted to know about everything around her. Already she felt the wind on her face and the smells of the river it carried. The sounds of gulls and the busy port were new and Fanny laughed imagining it all. It was fifty-five miles to the City and would take them most of two days, and she soon made friends with the friendly captain and his crew. Her mother was too seasick to come up on deck, but Fanny had no trouble at all. When the captain asked her to sing for them, she sang the ballad of the bachelors, a song the village children sang, and soon had them all laughing and clapping. Song followed song, and when it was over a cow that a farmer was taking down river began mooing loudly as if it were trying to sing. It turned out that the cow needed milking. That evening Mercy used the milk to make custard for everyone on board.

Afterwards Fanny sat on deck listening to the musical sound of the waves. Suddenly the setting sun shone so brilliantly on the waters that Fanny gasped. Though it was only the faintest gleams of colors Fanny saw, she knew she had seen them! As quickly as it had come that few seconds of color was gone, but Fanny had already stored it in her memory and she knew she would never ever forget that glimpse of colors.

Fanny could see nothing at all but she could hear it all, all of the city life around her. New York City was a noisy place, peddlers crying their wares, horses and wagons clomping on cobbled streets, and people everywhere. She was glad to step out of the busy street into the quiet of the eye doctor's office. The eye exam was long as two doctors examined Fanny's eyes.

"There is nothing we can do," doctor Mott had told her mother. "Poor child, she will always be blind." Fanny heard his words and felt the pat of his hand on her head, but she felt inside the way she always did. Whatever sight was she didn't need it at all.

The night they reached home Fanny heard her mother weeping, and then her Grandmother's words. "Now daughter, if the Lord does not give what you prayed for, then he knows that it is better for you not to have it."

That very week Fanny's mother got a new job as a housekeeper in the nearby town of North Salem. "Fanny," her mother said, "I have good news for you. We are to live together in my new employer's house. Your grandmother will come several times a week to visit, and you will have lots of other children in the village to play with. Most of the people in North Salem are Quakers and I think you will like it there."

Fanny didn't just like it there, she loved it! Soon she was speaking the plain language of the Quakers. One of the villagers kindly gave her rides on his wagon to the local mill, even on days when she invited herself. "No, thee ain't going with me," he would say some days, and Fanny was always sure he would give in when she said, "David, I tell thee I am going to mill with thee." Fanny would barely wait for his next words.

"Well, get thy bonnet and come along."

The Quaker church, The Society of Friends, was much more interesting than the church back home Fanny thought. The speaker barely stopped for breath in his sermons, and there were hymns! All the hymns told stories of sinners who died suddenly without hope. Anyone who had not repented and become a Christian could die anytime, children or grown-ups, without hope. Being ready to die was very important if one was to know for sure they were going to heaven. The hymns did make one think, and Fanny did love a good story even those about poor sinners.

Grandmother came often to teach her while her mother worked. Soon Fanny had memorized many parts of the Bible. She was nearly eight years old now, and life in North Salem should have been good the way it had been when they first came, but Fanny could feel inside that something had changed. Often people now told her, "Oh, Fanny, because you're blind you couldn't see anything if you did come with us." Or, "Fanny, you can't help with this because you're blind," or "that's not something you need to bother about since you can't go to school." Fanny began to wonder, and a little voice inside seemed to be telling her, "You are not like the children you play with. They can see and you can't." Whatever it was that sighted children had, she must not have it. And how could she learn the things she wanted without it? She began to feel sad.

Fanny knew what she had to do. She found her mother's rocking chair in the small room and knelt down next to it. It wasn't Grandmother's chair, but it would do. "Dear God," she prayed, "am I still your child even though I am blind? Your world is so big, God. Is there a little place you may have for me in your world?" It seemed to her that in the stillness of the room she suddenly knew that God was telling her in her heart, "Don't be sad, child. You are going to be happy and useful in your blindness." Fanny smiled. As Grandma said, "Troubles can be borne when God has good things ahead for you." She began a poem about a happy blind child.

The Landlady's Gift

Moving? "But I don't want to leave my friends," Fanny said. "We'll be so far away Grandma won't be able to come like she does here." Fanny stood rigid as her mother's arms came round her. "Why can't I stay here?"

Her mother's hand gently touched Fanny's face. "You know I can't give you up, Fanny, but I must take this new job, and you are coming with me. Now, please say no more about it." Fanny kept her tongue tight between her teeth so the words she wanted to say wouldn't pop out. Her mother had to be obeyed without argument, and was swift of hand when she wasn't. Her mother patted Fanny's shoulder. "Besides, child," she said, "your grandma will come sometimes, and I promise that you will get back to Southeast to visit often. Now we need to pack. We leave in the morning."

"This is it," the driver announced as the wagon came to a stop. "It's a right nice place, sits next to the village green," he said. "I reckon, little girl, you will soon make friends with the rest of the village children who play on the green." He lifted Fanny down and patted her head.

Her mother took her hand and led her to the front of the house. Fanny silently counted the steps they took until they stopped. She could feel her foot against wood and knew it must be a porch step.

"Fanny, we must climb three steps onto the porch of the boarding house," her mother announced. Fanny lifted her foot onto the step and silently counted, and kept counting her steps until they were across the porch. It was eight steps before her mother stopped and Fanny felt the wood of the door frame. "Mrs Hawley, we're here," her mother said as the door opened. The voice that welcomed them in was like what Fanny imagined a kind school teacher's might be. And Mrs Hawley the landlady who was to watch Fanny while her mother worked, very soon did take up where Grandma had left off teaching Fanny.

Fanny held Mrs Hawley's hand as they walked through the gardens outside the boarding house. "Now, Fanny, has your fine memory stored away all that I am telling you?" They had stopped at a bush of roses filling the air with a sweet smell.

"Yes, Mrs Hawley, I know the garden path well now, and where the flowers are. You have many rose bushes and we have stopped at one of the nicest to my nose and touch. I think these roses are bigger than all the others."

"You are right, Fanny. And you may pick all the other flowers when you wish, but you must not pick from this rose bush. These are white roses, the only ones in the garden and very special," Mrs Hawley said. "Now come and we will sit on the bench and begin today's lesson. It's time to memorize chapter three of Matthew." As Fanny sat down next to Mrs Hawley she could hear the pages of the large Bible rustling. Fanny was ready to listen to each line until she knew it perfectly. When they were done, Mrs Hawley closed the Bible. "You, child, have been gifted with a remarkable memory. I believe you will memorize the entire Bible." Like Grandma, Mrs Hawley was an old Puritan who believed in the Bible, every word of it. The church they attended was Presbyterian like the one Fanny had known at home in Southeast.

The church here was too poor to afford hymnals for the people, and so the deacons lined out the songs the way Fanny had heard the psalms lined in Southeast, but with one big difference. Here the deacons used songs from a collection of hymns and songs set to the musical style used in Europe, and there was a choir. In winter the Singing School teacher visited every week to teach young people from the new collection. Fanny was in the choir and loved it, though there were times when she struggled with the new hymns written by the deacons. But then the rest of the choir did too. Fanny had little patience when the words didn't fit the music where others she knew would have slipped into place perfectly. "Never mind," her friend Vet Main whispered one Sunday after they'd struggled through Deacon Jonah's newest hymn. "Deacon Jonah can't write all the songs. And you have a fine, sweet soprano voice, Fanny," he added.

They were walking the familiar path home, and Fanny turned her head away to hide the warmth that touched her face. "Vet, you're a true friend," she said, "or should I say one of the few friends I have left?"

After a moment of silence Vet said, "Well, you do win every Bible reciting contest in Ridgefield, and I mean all. Maybe it would help if you didn't enter every one. It's the same when you join every game on the green and you play to win. I sometimes think you have a chip on your shoulder just waiting for someone to dare you."

Fanny's thoughts raced. Because he was her friend Vet could say such a thing to her, but even he was close to going too far. Fanny stamped her foot. "You do understand," she said, "that I have to do what I do. I know that a blind person can do anything a sighted person can do if you give them a chance."

"Sorry," Vet said. "I guess you're right. Will I see you tomorrow then?"

"I'll be visiting school again tomorrow just in case the teacher has time for me."

But the next day came and went as usual and the teacher had no time at all to teach Fanny. She left discouraged and headed along the road to the boarding house. It was always the same. The other children learned to read and write, but there was no place in school for her to learn those things. She wanted desperately to learn.

Mrs Hawley did her best to see that Fanny did memorize the Bible. In two years Fanny had learned Genesis, Exodus, Leviticus, Numbers, the four Gospels and many psalms, Proverbs, Ruth, and the Song of Solomon. She never forgot any part of them. "How do you do it?" Mrs Hawley asked.

Fanny smiled. "When I want to read something from the Bible, I just turn a little button in my mind and there it is waiting for me." It was like there were little shelves in her mind and everything she ever learned was neatly stored there. Once she learned something she didn't forget, and she knew exactly where to find it when she needed it.

Mrs Hawley patted her hand. "Well child, your memory is a gift. Now shall I read you a fine new poem?"

"Please do," Fanny urged her. Mrs Hawley loved the Bible but she also loved good poetry and fine literature and shared them all with her. She often read her stories like the one about George Washington who cut down his father's cherry tree and truthfully confessed that he had done it. But Fanny wondered about that story. Had he really been such a good child? She knew she wasn't.

It was the white roses that caused her real downfall. One of the village girls, Lena, had come to visit Fanny and play in the garden. Fanny picked a few roses for her to take home. "Oh please, Fanny do pick some of those beautiful white roses," Lena begged.

"No," Fanny said. "We're not supposed to touch the white ones."

"I promise not to tell anyone," Lena said. "Just one will make this whole bunch so lovely. Please, please, Fanny."

"Well, just one," Fanny agreed. Feeling carefully with her hands she chose a large full rose from the bush that she knew was the white rose bush. "These smell better than all the other roses," she said handing it to Lena. She could not see the face of Mrs Hawley framed in the window closest to the garden.

Late that afternoon Mrs Hawley stopped Fanny in the hallway. "Fanny do you know who picked one of my white roses?" she asked.

"No, Mrs Hawley, I don't," Fanny lied. Mrs Hawley said no more and left for the kitchen. After supper the two of them sat down together for the reading Mrs Hawley liked to do with Fanny. This time she read the Bible story of Ananias and Sapphira who had both lost their lives because they lied. Fanny listened hard. Mrs Hawley didn't add a word to the story. She didn't have to, because Fanny had already determined she would never lie to her again. Mrs Hawley had given her the gift of learning the Bible and many other good things, and Fanny loved her. Still there was so much more to learn if only she could be like other children and go to school.

Fanny could think of nothing else these days but her need for school. "It's time you took that long face home for a visit to your grandmother. Let's hope she can put a smile back on it," her mother said.

Fanny was glad to hug her grandmother once again, and Grandpa too, but she didn't fool either of them. "Something is troubling you, child," Grandmother said that night. It was all Fanny could do to keep from tears as she told her grandmother everything on her heart.

"We need to ask our Heavenly Father for his help, child," Grandmother said as she drew Fanny down to kneel with her by the old rocking chair. Later when her grandmother had gone Fanny went to stand at the window. Every part of this room, of the whole house, was as familiar to her as if she had never left it. She knew it was night and imagined she could feel moonlight touching her head. Kneeling down she prayed: "Dear Lord, please show me how I can learn like other children." The soft chirp of a sleepy bird in a nearby tree made her smile, and it also made her remember. God cared for all he had made, birds and her. She would just wait. But this time Grandma would not be there to wait with her.

Summer came soon and with it news that brought Fanny and her mother hurrying home. Grandmother Eunice was ill. While her mother spoke in the kitchen with Grandpa, Fanny sat at her grandmother's side. Fanny's heart sank as the voice she loved so well whispered, "Grandma's going home. Soon I will be in heaven. Tell me, my dearest child, will you meet me in our Heavenly Father's house?"

Fanny could hardly speak. "By the grace of God, I will, Grandma," she said. Her grandmother drew her into her arms and prayed, and a short while later she died. Fanny's heart felt dark and heavy. She would miss Grandma so much, but how could she be sure she would see her again? Grandma and all the Crosby family believed that everyone needed to know the exact time they had been converted. They believed that the moment they had been saved was so powerful that it often moved a person to shout aloud or weep for joy. Fanny had never had a moment like that. She couldn't remember when she didn't believe in God, but neither could she point to a time when she knew she had been converted or saved. She didn't tell anyone.

Back in Ridgefield at the boarding house the other boarders tried to comfort Fanny and her mother. Mr Jacobs, a tailor who also played piano at the only Methodist church in town, was one of Fanny's favorites. Each Saturday after supper he played piano in the parlor for anyone who wanted to sing along, and for half an hour afterwards he taught Fanny to play. Tonight he played the most beautiful hymns Fanny had ever heard. At the end Mr Jacobs announced that anyone who wanted to hear more of Isaac Watts' hymns was most welcome to come to church with him tomorrow.

"Please, Mr Jacobs, may I come?" Fanny asked.

Mr Jacobs chuckled. "So, our little songbird likes our hymns. If it is alright with your mother you are welcome to come along." Turning to her mother he said, "Mrs Crosby, I believe Fanny has musical talent. She's already playing guitar at the Singing School, and doing very well on the piano. She might truly enjoy the music tomorrow."

Fanny pressed her mother's hand. "Please may I go? Mother?"

"Do let her go," Mrs Hawley urged. "And while we are speaking of Fanny's musical talents I should very much like her to attend the coming harpist recital in town with me on Friday afternoon."

"Well then, if I'm to have any peace I guess my answer is yes and yes again," her mother said. Before Fanny knew it she was playing piano, guitar, and even learning the harp. By the time she reached her teenage years she was already in demand to play and sing at local socials.

"You will bring your guitar to the picnic tomorrow," Vet asked as they walked home from choir practice at church.

"Yes," Fanny answered, "but not because you asked me, Vet. I've already promised Leah and Jane and Rachel that I would play. They're in charge of the program, you know." Fanny smiled.

"You, Fanny Crosby, no longer have a chip on your shoulder, but now that you are so popular at every social get-together you have a swelled head," Vet laughed and ducked Fanny's swatting hand. "And don't think we haven't heard about your story-telling talents with the younger children. I hear there isn't a whisper when you're telling them about pirates and robbers." They had come to the steps of the boarding house and as Fanny lightly went up the steps and was about to open the door, Vet called up to her. "But I've got to say your poem about that old scoundrel the miller was great. Too bad your mother wouldn't let Mr P. T. Barnum print the rest of the verses."

Fanny laughed and went inside. The poem about the cheating miller who mixed corn meal with his customer's flour nearly got her into trouble. She did love to write poems and there seemed to be so many things to write about, funerals, weddings, events, nature. But back in the room she and her mother shared, in the silence of the empty room the little nagging voice inside her began again. Vet and all the others she knew would go on to do the things in life they dreamed, but what about her? "I'm blind, and without an education. What kind of future is there for me?" It was the same question she'd asked God many years ago. The dreams she'd had as a little girl, all the things that she knew were somewhere out there in the world seemed far away now. The sound of footsteps, her mother's, hurried down the hall.

"Fanny, we're going back to North Salem. I've a new job there." Her mother hurried into the room and threw her arms around Fanny. "Remember how you loved the Quaker plain speech and all your friends there? I thought you would never stop using thees and thous when we moved here. And if I'm not mistaken you still have those old Quaker clothes packed away."

North Salem? Fanny's heart sank.

I Shall put her on the Mantel

Fanny put down the square she was knitting. She had learned to knit in Ridgefield and could do it now with barely a touch to guide her. Tomorrow was her fifteenth birthday. It would be a year since they'd come back to North Salem. Nothing had changed. "I'm still your blind child, God," she whispered, "and maybe that's all I can ever be."

"Fanny, Fanny, wonderful news," her mother's feet were running and she was shouting. Fanny's heart raced. Were they moving back to Ridgefield? She stood, dropping the knitting from her lap and ran to the door.

Her mother's arms were soon hugging her. "Fanny, you are going to school. At last there is a school for the blind in New York City and you can go. It's a fine new school where the blind are taught everything that the best schools teach. This is what you have dreamed of and longed for, Fanny, a real education."

"A school for the blind, and I'm to go there, to New York?" Fanny felt almost dizzy with the thought, and then just as suddenly she felt she couldn't stand still. With her arms around her mother she twirled them both until she had to stop. Fanny was sobbing with joy, or was it her mother or both of them? "God answered my prayer, Mother, I knew he would."

"I know you've never been away from home alone," her mother said. "And what shall I do without you, Fanny? I don't know."

"I just have to go, Mother. This will be the education I've longed for. We'll both be alright won't we?" Fanny didn't wait for an answer as she ran outside with a heart so full of joy and spilling over that she needed the whole outdoors to hold it. She could think of nothing else but the great adventure ahead of her. Her heart stayed light until the day came. She was to leave in the morning by coach with a woman who would travel with her to the city.

"Wake up, Fanny. I've let you sleep far too long. You need to dress and eat or you will be late." Her mother's hand shook Fanny awake. A sudden stab of fear went through Fanny's insides. Her hands were clumsy as she tried to dress hurriedly. At the table she could barely swallow any of the breakfast her mother served. The lump in her throat seemed the only thing holding back a sob. A knock at the door startled her. It was her traveling companion. Fanny rose quickly and felt for her bonnet and shawl. She had only a moment to hug her mother tightly and kiss her goodbye.

Her mother released her quickly and walked with her out to where the coach waited. "No time, child, for long goodbyes. Up you go, Fanny. You be a good girl and make us all proud, now," her mother said. Without a word, Fanny sat next to the woman, Miss Tolbright. As the coach pulled away to Norwalk where they would board the steamer, Fanny sat silent.

After an hour of silence Miss Tolbright who had tried to make conversation with Fanny gave up. After another hour Miss Tolbright could stand it no longer. "Young woman, you must tell me plainly. Do you want to go back home? I'm sure your mother is missing you too."

Fanny swallowed hard. She couldn't go back even though she desperately wanted to. "No, I must go on to school, thank you," she answered. Fanny felt a growing loneliness settle over her like a heavy blanket. Small fears made their way inside. Had she and her mother made a terrible mistake? She was glad when they reached the steamboat with its smells and sounds so different from the slow, gentle sailboat ride she had taken to New York City as a young child. There was no turning back now.

When they reached the city Miss Tolbright wished her well as she saw Fanny onto the coach hired to take her the rest of the short way to the Institute for the Blind. The driver was doing his best to talk to her. "Now, Miss, we're almost there, and it's a good thing you didn't have to hike through these acres of wet spring fields. Little tiny thing like you, might'a sunk right to the ankles in that there mud." He chuckled. As Fanny felt the coach slow and heard the sound of the horse's feet change their rhythm, her stomach lurched. This was it.

"Down you come, Miss," the driver said. "Let me tell you, this is one mighty fine building. Looks like a grand old mansion with lots and lots of windows and fancy roof and turrets. There appears to be plenty of garden space too, at least two acres. You can't see it, little Missy, but the whole place faces the river and rolling fields. It's mighty pretty. Here you go now, three steps right up to the porch, and looks like someone's already coming to take you in."

"Fanny managed to whisper a thank you to the kindly driver, and with her traveling bag in one hand, and the wooden steps before her feet, she began to climb, silently counting as she went. They were broad stairs and just as she reached the third, a cheery voice said. "That's the end of the steps, and straight ahead brings you right to the door. You must be Frances Crosby, our newest student, and I'm so glad to welcome you to the Institute." The cheerful voice belonged to someone tall with broad strong hands that Fanny felt as her luggage was taken from her by the woman. "I am Miss Lindborg, matron here," the woman said. "Let me take you upstairs to your new room and get you settled."

They crossed a hall and as they climbed a wide stairs, Fanny again counted them silently until they reached the top. "Three doors down on your right and we are there," Miss Lindborg said. "We have forty-one students, boy's rooms on the north side, girls on the south. Bedrooms are off limits during the daytime, but you'll be too busy having fun to be concerned about that dear."

Fanny listened as matron described the room she would share with some other girls, its shape, the window, her bed, her footlocker, the pegs for clothes, and the washbasins. As she sat on the large footlocker listening, picturing it, suddenly she heard nothing as all the newness and loneliness pressed in on her, and great sobs came.

Miss Lindborg's arms went round Fanny. "Oh, child, you've never been away from home before have you?" Fanny couldn't answer for sobbing. "Here comes our Mary one of the students who will be your guide today," Miss Lindborg said. "She will keep you company, dear, and answer any of your questions." Mary's soft voice began to soothe Fanny's fears and soon she was listening to Mary describe a typical school day.

"Matron is a kind person," Mary said, "but you don't want to linger when she comes to tell us it's time to rise and shine. First off, you need to get right to the washbasins, dress, make your bed, hang up your nightgown. We are responsible to keep our room neat, but when that breakfast bell rings we need to be downstairs and on our way into the dining room. If you are five minutes late, no breakfast!" Fanny couldn't help a chuckle and Mary laughed. "Girls enter the dining room to the right, boys to the left, and," Mary said, "you sure don't want to come in just as one of the boys begins to say grace for us. I'll show you how to find your way to the tables and give you a tour of the school too. A bell will ring at 8 a.m. for chapel, followed by study, and another bell to begin classes at 9 sharp. Afternoon classes go from 1.30 until 4.30. Between lunch and classes we are free to walk in the garden or study, or practice music. After supper at 7 sharp the whole school gathers to listen to the newspaper read. Evening chapel is at 8 p.m. and wonderful free time after that to have fun, just talk, or play games or sing, until 9.45 for prayers and bedtime. Fanny you will love it!" Mary said. "Do you mind if I call you Fanny?" Mary asked as she impulsively reached to take Fanny's hand in hers. Fanny squeezed Mary's hand gently letting her know that she didn't mind. Mary's touch had let Fanny know too that here was someone she wanted for a friend.

"Not a bit," Fanny said. "It's what everyone calls me at home. Mary, I think we shall be friends, and I can already tell that you are among the kindest, gentlest persons I've met." Fanny smiled and lifted her free hand to touch Mary's face. Mary did the same and they were soon laughing and telling each other all the little details they knew, like the color of their hair and eyes, their favorite foods, the music they both loved, and favorite things to do. Fanny's heart began to lighten, and by the time they left for the noon meal she was ready to face meeting others and being the newcomer at school.

That night Fanny fell asleep on her narrow bed still thinking of all the new information that was now stored in her memory ready to use. She was here at the Institute, and she knew it would be everything she had longed for.

Fanny loved learning! She was beginning to understand history, philosophy, English grammar, the Bible and science from her teachers. There were maps and globes of the world with raised lines and prominences that she could feel and understand, and books with embossed letters. She could hardly wait for Dr Russ, the superintendent's class, when the good man read literature to them, an hour that never seemed too long to her. Like Fanny, Dr Russ loved poetry and read them the best of poets.

The method the teachers used for their lessons was simple. The teacher read the lesson twice, three times if needed, and the students repeated it. The following day all students were required to recite the lesson in their own words. Fanny loved the grammar book and soon felt at home with it, including its section on verse. From childhood her memory had been her library and now it held all that she gave it so that she could easily recall and recite even the whole or any part of the grammar book. Only one thing stumped her, like a stone wall that she could not get past, the awful subject of math.

Dear Anna, who had become a close friend was the student assigned to tutor her in math. "Oh, Anna," Fanny said after their third day on multiplication, "you have managed to pull me through addition and subtraction, but I just cannot do this multiplication and you know I will fail division miserably." Even with special metal type and grooved boards to place them on, Fanny could barely do math.

Anna put her arms around Fanny's shoulders. With her cheek against Fanny's she could feel tears running down Fanny's face. "You have tried so hard," Anna said, "and you are so bright in everything else, and I don't understand it, but I think we need to face the truth that math seems impossible for you. I will go and talk to Dr Russ about it, Fanny."

Anna returned from superintendent Russ's office just as the dinner bell rang and found Fanny about to go into the dining room. Gently she took Fanny's hand in hers. "Oh, Fanny, Dr Russ says that you simply must learn the multiplication tables or else." Fanny heard the hesitation in Anna's voice. "Or else he says if you do not learn them before my next report he will come himself and put you on the mantel shelf. It's a very big shelf and you are quite small," she added.

Fanny's heart sank. She could barely imagine such a thing. But Dr Russ loved his school and his students and would do everything he could to see them succeed. "Then I must just do this, Anna. After our meal can we try again, please?"

Fanny learned the multiplication tables, but she could go no further! For the first time she discovered something she could loathe completely and wrote her feelings in a small poem,

> I loathe, abhor, it makes me sick
>
> To hear the word arithmetic!

Finally, Anna realized that Fanny simply could not get division. She reported to Dr Russ that Fanny's was a hopeless case when it came to math. This time even he agreed that Fanny would be excused from math and concentrate on the rest of her classes. At the good news, Fanny hugged Anna and twirled her round, overjoyed with her freedom from the hated subject. Already a poem was forming in her mind and soon on her lips. This was something Fanny could not help doing. Even as a child she had made poems about things like the wind in the flowers, the song the brook sang, events around her, poems for funerals, poems about people like the bad miller back home, and since coming to the Institute it seemed the poems came as easily as ever, more so than ever.

"Fanny, Fanny you must write a poem about the mouse Mr Brown found tangled in his hair when he woke up this morning," one of the girls urged. She did, and then she wrote a poem about two of the teachers who were clearly in love with each other. She wrote poems about events in the newspapers, poems for class, and more poems. Soon Fanny was the one asked to make a poem to welcome any important visitors to the school. At every exhibit the school held to show the public what a fine education could do for the blind, Fanny was always part of the program reciting her poetry. When a new building was added to the Institute, Mr Reiff the music teacher asked Fanny to write the words for a march for the celebration. Fellow students wanting to write poetry now sought Fanny's help, and often they would meet secretly in little groups gathered at night in Fanny's room. Fanny was all too willing to perform and to help lesser writers. It was beginning to show.

"You are wanted in Mr Jones' office, Fanny," Matron informed her. Fanny hurried down to the office where the new superintendent waited. He probably wants me to write a new poem for another important visitor, she thought, but what waited for her was something quite different, something she would not want to hear.

The Shape of her Head Will Tell

Fanny went straight down the hall to Mr Jones. She knew her way so well she was often asked to take visitors on a tour of the Institute. It could be that someone important was coming and Mr Jones had called for her to prepare a welcome. Everyone seemed to like her poems, even the ones she wrote on short notice for friends and sometimes unexpected guests to the school. Mother had told her that Grandpa walked four miles to get a copy of the newspaper with a poem she'd written for it. Fanny smiled thinking of dear old Grandpa and the folks like Mrs Hawley who often shared her poems with others. Celebrating public events, writing eulogies for funerals, poems for the annual exhibit at the Institute, and in between for most other school functions did keep her busy, but she loved doing it all. She knew by her finger's touch that she had arrived at Mr Jones office and the door was open. She stood a moment waiting for Mr Jones to speak.

"Fanny, come in and close the door behind you, please." Mr Jones' grave tone of voice puzzled her as Fanny found the seat exactly where she knew it would be.

"My dear, it has come to my notice that we must talk about your poetry writing. You have written a number of poems of merit, but your talent is still crude and undeveloped. If it is ever to amount to much you must learn to smooth and polish your verses. You must study and learn all you can if you are to reach a higher standard. I know you are acquiring a reputation among some of your fellow students, but remember, Fanny, you cannot accept flattery, even from a friend. Whatever talent you possess, child, belongs wholly to God and you ought to give him the credit for all that you do."

Fanny felt the burning touch of his words on her heart. He was speaking truly to her and she knew it. She swallowed hard, past the lump forming in her throat.

"Have I wounded your feelings, Fanny?" Mr Jones' voice was full of concern and kindness.

Fanny could not help her impulse to reach out to him. "Oh, Mr Jones, you have only spoken to me the way a father would. I thank you, truly." After a few more words of advice, Fanny was excused. It was all she could do to keep from wailing as she hurried down the hall. The day was warm and most everyone would be out strolling in the gardens at this hour, and she needed to be alone. The nearest large empty parlor would do. Fanny rushed into the room and bumped straight into a very plump housemaid.

"Fanny, me lass, now whatever is the matter?"

Fanny leaned her head into Molly's broad chest and sobbed. The house maid led her to the nearest piano bench and held her close while she wept. Little by little Fanny quieted as the kind woman smoothed her hair and murmured soft Irish words of comfort.

"It's nothing, except that I've let myself be fooled into thinking I was somebody I'm not. You know what I mean. I'm sort of like a little frog with a big voice who thinks he is quite the biggest frog in the pond?"

The housemaid laughed heartily. "Well now, I'm thinking that little frog might have had a bit of a come down, like a certain young lass." She took Fanny's hand in her own, "Ah, lass, as me dear mother used to say, the good Lord isn't finished with you yet. He gives each of us gifts meant just for us, and I've heard you playing your guitar, singing, and playing piano, and some of us maids have heard a poem or two of yours. Under those black curls of yours there's a fine mind, lass. You tell that little frog of yours to cheer up for old Molly." Fanny wiped her eyes and promised to do her best.

Molly's words made Fanny smile a little as she thought of them, but Mr Jones' words came again and her smile quickly fled. By bedtime Fanny knew what she would do. She had told only Anna and Mary what had happened in Mr Jones's office, and both promised to say nothing to anyone as Fanny put her new plan into place. She would write and from now on she would pay no attention to flattery. She would learn to smooth and polish her poetry no matter how much work it took. It was her duty. Hadn't Mr Jones said that every gift was from God? On her knees at her bedside for prayer time, she whispered, "Thank you, God, for everything, and especially poetry." Classes seemed to fly by, and Fanny thought little of it when her teachers began to insist on her paying more attention to the lessons and less to poetry. Hadn't she promised herself to work harder on her poetry? When she was again summoned to Mr Jones she didn't dare to imagine what it was for this time.

"Fanny, I'm sorry to say," Mr Jones began, "but your grades are slipping down and you are not doing well in your courses. I must insist that you write not another line of poetry, not one, for the next three months."

Three months! Fanny's mind whirled. She had to obey Mr Jones, but how? Week after week as she tried to concentrate on her classes, little things like a word, a line, a picture would slip into her mind, and begin to turn into a poem. A teacher would call on her and Fanny had no idea what had been said. It was far worse in music class with Mr Reiff, when feelings just flowed out of her heart in poems the music seemed to call from her, songs waiting to be sung. It was hopeless and by the end of six weeks Fanny knew very well why she was called once again to Mr Jones' office.

"Fanny, your grades are worse than ever," Mr Jones said. "Can you tell me why?"

"Sir, I try but my head gets so full of words, of poems that I must not write and I cannot keep away, that I don't know what to do." Fanny couldn't think of any excuses, she was failing her lessons and it was her own fault. But what Mr Jones said next could not be true. Was she hearing him right?

"Well, Fanny, it seems you truly are a poet, and I cannot keep you from writing your poems. You may go on with your poetry, but you must promise me to pay attention to your lessons and learn all you can." Fanny could not thank him enough and nearly skipped down the hall to her friends. She was free to write, free to learn, free to be herself once more.

Before the year was out the whole school was excitedly awaiting the coming of the famous Mr George Combe, lecturer and teacher of the latest science of Phrenology, the study of the shape and texture of the head. Anna could hardly wait. "Just think of it, Fanny, they say he can tell by feeling your head what you may become in the future. My mother writes that all of New York City is talking about the new science and the great Mr Combe. Oh, Fanny, I wonder if he will feel your head?"

Fanny laughed. "And if he does, what will he say, that I shall grow up to play piano in some country church, or become a knitter of fine shawls?" She did not dare to say out loud even to Anna, "Or may I be one day a real poet?"

Mr Combe had been exactly right when he examined the head of one of the boys and declared him a fine mathematician. The boy was noted for being able to calculate things like the number of seconds two persons had lived given the days months and years of their lives, and do it while listening to two people's conversations and singing a song.

When Mr Combe came to Fanny she held her breath. "Yes," the great man said as he examined Fanny's head in front of the whole school. "This young lady is a poet. You must give her all the help you can, the best of books, let her converse with poets, and one day she will make her mark in the world." Fanny nearly forgot to breathe! In the days that followed Mr Combe's visit, Fanny's life took a new turn. Mr Jones was now eager to do everything he could to help Fanny with her talent.

One of the board members of the Institute, Mr Hamilton Murray was known to be a fine teacher of poetry. "I shall teach you, Fanny, but you will not find me an easy teacher," he said, "for I will demand the very most from you and expect you to work hard." He was true to his word.

Fanny grew to listen to every word that Mr Murray read from long poems and was required to commit them to memory. She learned rhyme, rhythm, and meter, and Mr Murray quickly pointed out where her poems lacked these. He read poems from the best known poets to her and made her imitate them each in poems of her own. "It is called paraphrasing," he said, "a good beginner's tool." And he was strict, as Fanny soon learned.

"Well, Fanny, have you written your paraphrase of Nathaniel Willis's poem yet?" The morning had gone by quickly and Fanny hadn't yet done her assignment. "It is now eleven forty-five, Fanny, and you know lunch is at twelve," he said. "You do understand, Fanny that no verses will mean no dinner," he added. By noon Fanny had finished her assignment.

"I see that you have learned how to compose a poem well when you put your mind to it."

Soon Fanny's poems were once more in demand for every exhibit and special event at the school, like the Ladies' Fair held for three days between Christmas and New Year to raise money for the school. She had become one of the star pupils representing the school to the public. That the blind could be educated and have a useful future was still a new thing, and many distinguished visitors including presidents and generals, famous people like Jenny Lind the Swedish nightingale, musicians, and others came to see for themselves how the school functioned. Fanny was thrilled to meet them, officially welcome them, listen to them, and write about them. On the day that one of her favorite poets, William Cullen Bryant came, Fanny listened with awe as he read his own poetry. It was Fanny's duty to guide Mr Bryant on a tour of the school.

At the end of the tour of the school gardens, Mr Bryant asked Fanny if they might sit for a few moments on one of the garden benches. As they sat, he said, "Miss Crosby, I have long wanted to meet the young woman behind the poems I have enjoyed reading in the papers as well as magazines. I want to encourage you, young lady, to keep up the good work." Fanny couldn't believe her ears! He talked to her for the next few moments pointing out things from her work that he had especially liked. When he left Fanny was sure she would never forget a single word he had said, and she would remember this as one of the best moments of her life! In bed that night Anna and she talked far into the night.

A sleepy Anna said, "You'll be writing poems for everything now I'm sure. You are so much more passionate for great causes than I am, Fanny. Every night when we listen to the newspapers read, you come away ready to defend some cause to the last. Sometimes, I am so weary from a long day trying to help the young ones that I find myself nodding off during the news."

"Oh, Anna, you are the smartest, most energetic teacher those little ones could have. I know now that I'm assisting teaching the younger students it isn't so easy."

"Mmm," was Anna's only reply, soon followed by a light snoring. Fanny smiled, it was the one thing she never told Anna about: her snore. It was not exactly musical but sort of so to Fanny's ears.

Fanny had just turned eighteen, and there was news from home. As Fanny listened to her teacher, Mr Chamberlain, reading the rest of her letter from her mother she clapped for joy. There could be no finer news! Fanny's mother was getting married again.

"He sounds like a fine man, too, a widower with a son, which means you will have a new half-brother," her teacher added. Fanny had never known her own father who had died before she was a year old. Excitement and pleasure ran through her as she thought of the coming wedding, a step-father, and a brother all at once! Her beloved mother was to be a bride again. Fanny could hear the words of a wedding poem already forming in her mind, but they were quickly interrupted as the door flew open.

"Fanny, there you are. I am so glad you are still here." It was Mr Jones' voice, and in it she heard urgency. "Fanny, the President has just arrived unexpectedly at the school and is in the reception room. Can we count on you, Fanny, to give a welcome poem for the President of the United States? I'm afraid you will only have fifteen minutes to prepare. Do you think you can put that mind of yours to work on a poem? I am sure Mr Chamberlain will not object to letting you use his office. The chapel bell will ring in fifteen minutes, and I should like you to be first on the program to welcome President Tyler."

Fanny swallowed hard. "President Tyler is here, and I have fifteen minutes to get ready?" Excitement or something like it gripped her and already her mind was thinking of how to welcome the President of the United States. "I'll do my best," she managed to say.

"Wonderful," Mr Jones said, "shall we leave her to it then, Mr Chamberlain?" Fanny barely heard the two men leave and the door close behind them.

Her mind was whirling. Quickly Fanny folded her hands and bowed her head, "Please, dear God, help me to use the gift you've given me to honor this great man, the President of our country." Soon lines came and then stanza after stanza picturing the greatness of America and the task before President Tyler, the man chosen to lead. When the bell for chapel sounded, Fanny sighed, the new poem was beautiful and fully formed and ready in her mind to give it.

Mr Jones led Fanny onto the platform and introduced her as the Institute's Poet in Residence. Fanny scarcely heard his words and thought only of the poem she was about to share. When she finished, the applause was loud, and afterwards many praised the poem. Fanny smiled and said her thanks. She too was thinking the poem had been a good one. She remembered how she had prayed as a little child to ask God if he had any place in his world for a poor blind girl, and all along he had been planning for her. The little poems she'd made up back then were really the beginning of her becoming a poet, and at last here at the Institute she was learning to polish and smooth that gift.

Anna had come to walk with her, and as they linked arms, she said, "Fanny, you must not think me a flatterer, but your poem today was so beautiful I felt tears on my face."

Fanny pressed Anna's hand, "Oh, Anna, I thought it was beautiful too, and please do not think I am flattering myself. A poem can come that way almost by itself."

"Yes," Anna said, "but it is a gift few of us are given." "By the way," she added, "I nearly forgot to tell you it looks like the secret is out. We're really going on a canal trip. The board of managers has approved and hired a boat to take us. Didn't you tell me one of your childhood dreams was to be a sailor? Well, it looks like you're going to be one after all, Fanny."

Fanny laughed. "Then we will be sailors together disguised as passengers, and no one will guess our secret."

Anna chuckled. "Well, I know I shall be wearing my best traveling dress and carrying a new shawl of softest wool. I will expect you to look every bit as fine."

"I promise to try," Fanny said. "If there is still time, I think I must get a letter off to my mother before Mr Chamberlain leaves his office. She will love hearing about the poem and the boat trip, even though it means I won't be going home for vacation."

The Blind Girl's Poem

Fanny's heart sang as she dictated a short letter to her mother. "So, Mother dear, I will miss you and think of you often, but I know you will be glad for me sailing all the way to Niagara Falls, all twenty of us. We will have sighted teachers going with us, so I'm sure to learn a lot, and will write you as soon as we are back. Have a lovely summer, Mother, and my love to all. That's it, Mr Chamberlain, thank you."

"Off with you then, Miss Fanny. I know you do enjoy your meals, and you won't want to miss your last dinner on land for awhile." Fanny could hear the smile in Mr Chamberlain's voice. She guessed the whole school knew by now about the silly poem she'd written on how much she truly loved good food. She did have a large appetite, though she never seemed to grow a bit taller or put on a single ounce these days!

At the dining room Anna and Mary were waiting for her. Though all three girls were the same age, Fanny was by far the shorter and smaller framed. Ceily, one of the young Irish housemaids had told them how Anna's golden hair gleamed in its tightly bound bun, and Mary's hair was thick and dark like Fanny's black curls. By gentle touch each knew the face of the others, and from the beginning the three had been fast friends. Fanny needed no one to tell her that it was Mary waiting as the sweet, faint odor of lilacs, the scent of Mary's favorite powder reached her. Fanny knew instantly from their voices who was speaking. It was Anna who called out, "Fanny over here by the doorway." Fanny followed her voice.

They were just in time to slip in before grace was announced. As Fanny sat down and felt the edges of her plate, she whispered to Anna who sat next to her, "Remind me never to write another poem on how much I love mealtimes, even Mr Chamberlain seems to know about it," she said.

"Well, if you think that's bad,"Anna said, "as I passed the parlor this morning, Molly said, 'Good morning, Miss Anna', and seconds later someone called out, 'There goes Anna, one of the watermelon girls.' I couldn't make out who it was, but are they going to remind us every summer of that awful prank you dreamed up, Fanny?"

Fanny laughed. "I do take the blame for that one. But we did confess taking that watermelon while poor old Mr Stebbins took a nap. And we did think they owed us at least a taste from the school's melon garden before they were all sold off. Who could have dreamed that the cook planned to give everyone a taste the very next day!"

Mary on Fanny's other side, said, "Ah, Fanny you may have confessed that one, but I doubt the poor postman will ever figure out who hid his book and pen so often, or who left him a poem telling him he shouldn't deliver mail in the rain or he'd catch cold and you'd have the nurse make him flax tea. I fear there is an impish streak in your nature, Miss Crosby, and I do hope it isn't catching."

Fanny was enjoying her meal of cold meat and summer salad. Between bites she said, "All that's past. Each of us is far too old for such pranks now. But I do still love a good joke."

Anna chuckled. "So long as we don't all three of us land in trouble again," she said.

"By the way, Fanny," Mary asked, "have you planned what poem you will use and what music you will sing and play as we travel? Mr Jones is expecting me to do my usual thing: be ready for questions on literature and history to show how well the Institute is doing to educate the blind. Of course we know what you will be doing, Anna, star student of our mathematical department."

Fanny swallowed her last bit of bread and jam. "I don't know yet what poem I should use, but I have thought I'd sing the song I made for Mr Reiff's new music, the piece he played for us yesterday. I can play it on the harp or the piano."

"Yes," Mary said, "but don't forget you need to let Mr Reiff know by tonight what you are going to do. Can you believe we're going in the morning? I think I won't sleep a bit tonight."

The school's rule not to return to one's room during the day was set aside so that students going on the trip could pack their things. Fanny was on her way to her room when she thought she heard something coming from farther down the hall. She stood still and listened. Someone was crying, the kind of sound that only hard sobbing makes. Fanny hurried down the hall. When she reached the door she knocked and waited. The sobbing stopped and a voice said, "Go away, please." Lucy, it was Lucy!

Fanny opened the door. "It's me, Fanny," she said, closing the door behind her. "What is it, Lucy?" As Lucy wept again, Fanny made her way to where she sat on the chest at the foot of her bed. Kneeling beside the girl, she put her arms around her and rocked her gently.

After a while, Lucy swallowed hard and brushed the tears from her face. "I know you and the others are going tomorrow on your trip up the Erie canal, and I'm glad for you, really. I just sometimes think I'll never be welcome anywhere outside this Institute where no one can see me." She sighed deeply.

Fanny smoothed Lucy's scarred brow, feeling once again the terrible ridges left by the gun that had exploded in Lucy's face gouging out her eyes and leaving her badly scarred. "To me, and to the rest of us here," she said, "you, with your loving heart and gentle hands are the one with a beautiful soul, and when you sing it's like listening to a sweet bird from an enchanted land. How the young children love to hear you, and they would rather learn their lessons from you, than any of us. If they could suddenly see tomorrow, they have learned to love you so well, it would not make any difference to them. They would see you with their hearts, as I do. Whatever is ahead, Lucy, my dear old grandmother used to say that God gives what he knows is best for us, and we can ask him anything. He has something good for you to do, I know it. He has brought you here for a reason, just the way he brought me."

"I wanted to go with all of you, so much," Lucy said, "but I know that people aren't going to want to see such a monstrous face as I have. The whole point of the trip is to get people to see what an education can do for the blind. All that would be lost with one look at my face."

Fanny tightened her arms around Lucy. "I will tell you everything you missed on this trip, Lucy, every detail as I see them through the eyes of those who can see, and all that I hear and feel besides. Now, I want to lend you one of Mr Reilly's new books, you know the one with raised letters, a book of wonderful poems that can open a world of places for you to visit. Stay right here while I get it."

When Fanny returned with the book, Lucy took it and handed a small lace-edged handkerchief to Fanny in exchange. "My aunt gave me this," she said. "Take it and think of me." The two hugged and Fanny hurried off. She must still work on the poem she would need to recite at the end of each exhibit in the towns and villages along the canal. People had to learn what an education could do for the blind. She thought of Lucy, not only blind but with a face so deeply scarred. Lines began to form in her mind.

> *But there's a lamp within whose sacred light*
> *Burns with a luster ever pure and bright—*
> *'Tis education we have shown to you*
> *What by its rays illumed, the blind can do.*
>
> *Without it, life a dreary waste would be*
> *With nought to break its long monotony—*
> *No sunny beams to light our cheerless way—*
> *Our vacant thoughts, ah! Whither would they stray?*
>
> *But thanks to God, his sovereign care we own,*
> *He hath not left us friendless and alone.*
> *His pitying eye beheld the helpless blind,*
> *And reared us friends affectionate and kind.*

Fanny felt a tear run down her face. Education, learning did bring light and open the mind to see what blind eyes couldn't. What would have become of her, of all of them at the Institute if there was no such place as a school for the blind? By evening she had written it in her mind, ready to use it everywhere she would need to speak.

It was time. Fanny and Anna and Mary stood in line waiting their turn to board the George Washington canal boat that would be their home for the next few days. "It's a fine packet boat, Miss Landry," one of the sighted teachers announced. "The cabin runs to what's called the bow deck, the space in front of the boat where there are seats for those who want to sit outside.

At the back of the cabin is another deck called the stern deck where the steersman work. This boat also has a deck on top of the cabin with a small railing around it, and you all know that when we are allowed to go up top we must strictly obey the captain's orders."

"Yes, yes," came answering cries from all around Fanny. "When you hear the order, 'low bridge' you fall flat, face down and hold still until the all clear is given." Fanny knew that some of the bridges on the canal were so low that sometimes passengers who didn't flatten themselves to the deck were swept off into the water or worse.

Fanny walked up the wooden walkway as the voice of the Captain said, "Watch your step, Miss," and a moment later a large hand under her elbow helped her up the walkway. Inside the cabin even Fanny couldn't tell who was where in the jumble of voices and noises coming from every direction. At last Mr Reilly managed to still the crowd. "Now, ladies, your quarters are in the front of the cabin, the bow side, and gentleman to the stern. The cabin is long and narrow, with windows on most of the wall space. Down the center is a narrow table where our meals will be served. At night the benches will be unfolded to make cot beds, and above the cots will be upper berths which hook into the boat's sides and are suspended on the other side by ropes from hooks in the ceiling. It is all quite safe and well thought out. At night a large thick curtain will be lowered between the ladies' and the gentlemen's quarters." Miss Landry will lead you girls now on a tour of your quarters, show you where the washbasins are and where you may store your things. I shall do the same for the gentlemen."

When all the laughter and questions had finally died down, Miss Landry took her group of girls out to the bow deck. "Now if you promise to stay seated here with Miss Smith she will be not only your history teacher, but will describe everything we pass, because we are about to leave port!"When the excitement once again died down, Miss Landry made an offer that went straight to Fanny's heart. "If any of you wish to brave going up top with me, I will take you now. Only four of the less adventurous girls stayed below while Fanny and the rest followed Miss Landry. Fanny could feel the sunshine on her face, hear the sounds of a busy canal port, and smell the peculiar aroma of canal life, smells of fish and boats and more.

Every day was a wonder, full of fun and learning too. Miss Landry and the other teachers did not let any chance for teaching go by. Fanny knew more now about New York state than she had ever known. At the locks, box-like parts of the canal where the boats were lifted down or up by water let into the canal, all the students and teachers left the boat to walk on the towpath for exercise. Fanny had been laughing at something Anna said and did not hear the Captain step up to help her down the last step to shore. "Why thank you, Captain," she said as he took her arm. She could tell he was wearing his uniform jacket with the rough braided cuff.

"Don't know how you knew it was me, Miss," he said. "I'd never have believed a boatload of blind passengers would get around the way you do. I thought this might be a kind of a quiet somber trip this time, but you all are some of the liveliest, happiest passengers this boat has seen." Fanny smiled and thanked him.

Mary squeezed Fanny's arm as they walked together along the tow path with the others. "I heard that boy mule driver whistling as we passed. Miss Landry says they are a rowdy bunch, and some of them no older than twelve. Can you imagine spending all your days driving the mules that pull the canal boats and only going to school when the canal freezes if you get to go at all?"

"No," Fanny said. "I heard too, that sometimes the poor hogees, as the Captain calls them, are not well treated, and sometimes a bad captain cheats them out of their pay. It's not fair, and it's no wonder they have a reputation for fighting."

"True," Anna said, "and I reckon that a boy like that dreams of the day he might own his own boat and be a captain."

"Well, if I were a captain," Fanny said, "I would see that he did." Anna chuckled. It was just the sort of cause Fanny would take on.

Fanny slept well on her boat cot, and ate with her usual hearty appetite the large meals served them.

At every stop their boat was welcomed by people waiting to take them to the schools or churches where crowds had come to see the blind students perform. Fanny knew that among them were parents with blind children, and hoped with all her heart that some of them would be moved to send their children to the Institute. They were nearing the end of their tour, and Fanny could feel the excitement in the air. They would soon be visiting the mighty Niagara Falls!

Two hours before the boat docked in Buffalo, Miss Landry gathered them all for a final lesson on the great Niagara Falls. "We will visit Goat Island right by the American side of the falls," she said. "The story goes it was so named for the poor goat that a farmer left there to pasture over the summer, but before he could row back for it the weather changed and that poor goat never came home." Fanny listened carefully as Miss Landry gave facts and figures about the amounts of water that rushed over the cliffs above the falls. She tried to imagine the giant water falls as her teacher described it, but nothing could have prepared her for the real thing.

At last she was standing next to Anna and Mary along with the rest of the students and staff on Goat Island, close to the mighty thunder of waters pouring down from the high cliffs. She could taste the mist in the air, and standing so near the falls, its roaring power surrounded her like a living thing whose sound she would never forget.

On the way home, back to the Institute, the girls sat on the stern deck for their last hours on the canal. This time they did not stop along the way. Traffic on the canal was as busy as ever, and their teachers told them about the great loads of goods that passed them as they traveled. "I have so much to tell Lucy," Fanny said.

"Oh, how will you tell her about the falls, how can anyone imagine such a powerful thing if they haven't visited it?" Mary asked.

"I know I can only try," Fanny agreed. "It seemed like thunder one moment and the next like the most powerful music."

Anna sighed, before she said, "Well then, Fanny, I think you will have to write a poem about the falls." Miss Landry was already calling them to gather inside the cabin. "Looks like your poem will have to wait, Fanny. We're about to land."

Just Too Busy

That night back at the Institute, Fanny wrote a poem about the falls. As she told it to Lucy, the words formed a picture in her own mind, and she could hear Lucy's deep intake of breath as she too must have pictured the crashing waters. "Oh my," Lucy said as Fanny finished. "You made it seem so real, Fanny, I thought I could feel the spray on my face and hands. Will you come and say it for the children? I know they will love it."

Fanny smiled. "If you like. Let's get them together with my students to hear it," she said. "Sometimes, I can hardly believe that I'm instructing the younger children now," she added. "It seems so short a time ago that I was a fifteen-year-old blind girl starting my own first day of lessons here at the Institute."

Lucy's soft fingers touched Fanny's arm lightly. "Soon you'll be able to graduate but I'm glad the school wants you to stay on as a teacher. We need you so much."

"Well, it looks like I'll be hired, and it's what I want to do, teach and write. But sometimes I'm so busy performing at school events, welcoming visitors, being the school's tour guide, studying, and tutoring my little class of students, I think I won't be able to write another poem," she said as the two walked down the hall.

"Oh Fanny, that will never happen," Lucy said. "I've heard that you are up every night until one or two in the morning working on your poems. No matter what else you do poetry is a part of you that just seems to spill out. It's like a deep well that doesn't ever run dry, only it's in your heart."

Fanny thanked her with a light squeeze of Lucy's hand. "Lucy, that is a beautiful thing to say." For a moment the only sound was their footsteps. Lucy's made a tiny metallic sound from the nailed heels of her shoes. Fanny's made a slight squeak against the wooden floor. Though she was small and light, she walked the way she did everything, ready to take on the world!

If only she could be as sure of other things. "I wish my dear old grandmother had lived to see this place and what it's done for me," Fanny said. "I wish too you could have known her, Lucy. My grandmother was everything to me. She taught me Bible stories, how to pray, how to trust that God hears our prayers and always does what is best for us." Fanny slowed her steps for a moment. "In her last words to me she asked me if I would see her in heaven. I told her, "Grandma, I hope so." Sometimes I think about her and ask myself that same question again, will I see her in heaven? I hope so. I just wish I could be sure. My Grandmother was sure she was going to heaven, and that's the part I'm still missing. Her ancestors came over on the *Mayflower*, and Grandmother had their same strong faith and courage, besides which she dearly loved me. I wish you'd known her, Lucy."

Lucy was quiet for a moment. "I had a mother who taught me to pray when I was a little girl. Mother sometimes said heaven was where my grandpa had gone, and as a child I just accepted that. Everyone went to church, and back then I didn't have any questions, I guess." Once more Lucy was quiet, and then Fanny heard her take a deep breath. "But after the accident to my eyes," Lucy said, "I didn't want to go to church. I didn't want to listen to anyone tell me about a God who hadn't protected me. I was angry, and I even blamed God for what happened. It took a long time, Fanny, before I knew that God still loved me. Now when I get down and sorry for myself, he sends someone like you, Fanny, to cheer me up. I'm sorry I'm not much help with things like being sure who will go to heaven, but if it comes from being good, then you surely will be there, Fanny."

"Lucy, no one could be as good as you," Fanny said. "Maybe one of these days I'll have time to think more about it all. Meanwhile there's work calling us. Let's find Anna and Mary."

June arrived with warm days and the sweet smell of lilacs coming from the school gardens. It was vacation time, but there would be no vacation for Fanny this year. The school day was over and students hurrying to meet friends in the garden passed Fanny and Anna who were going the other way. Anna clutched Fanny's arm as someone bumped her shoulder. "Sorry," a male voice said. "I'm usually not so clumsy, I just didn't think there might be somebody on the opposite side of the hallway." Fanny laughed lightly as she listened to the young man's steps retreating into the distance. They had just come from a meeting with the superintendent and several of the managers, and she and Anna had been so busy talking they hadn't even heard him coming.

"Fanny, I've never been this nervous before," Anna said. "I can't believe we will be performing in front of all those important people at one time. The whole New York State Senate is coming to visit our school."

"We'll just have to be the proper young ladies they expect, and do the best we can." Fanny wasn't nervous yet, but she was excited. "Think of what their support could do to help our school," she said.

"Fanny," Anna said, "if any of us does nearly as fine as you always do, we'll be glad. You're not only our star poet, but you can sing, play the harp, the piano, and the organ."

"Oh, Anna, I know you will do well. Nobody is as good a mathematician as you are. It's a great chance to impress them. In less time than you can imagine it will all be over. And then we will be off to spend the summer riding wagons to out-of-the-way places, bringing our exhibitions to churches and towns wherever they'll have us. And who knows what kinds of hotels we'll be staying in. Hopefully, it will be worth it all to make the school known." Fanny stood still for a moment. "I think I won't mind however far we have to go, or whatever kinds of places they put us up in, if it helps change people's minds about the blind. There are still so many who believe that nothing much can be done for a blind child." Her heart always remembered the longings of her own childhood to go to school, to learn, and have her dreams fulfilled. "It makes me angry to think of all the blind children whose lives are miserable because their parents are so sure there is no hope for them."

The hardness of the trip upstate took all of Fanny's determination to keep her going. The wagon travel was rough, the hotels sometimes poor, and the constant performing tiring. "If I have to answer another dumb question about blind people, I think I will make up the worst answers I can think of," Fanny said one night.

"Well at least we get to laugh a bit. Mr Reiff, who sees perfectly, surely turned the tables on that hotel clerk who thought he was one of the blind students. When the clerk asked him how long he had been that way," Anna mimicked Mr Reiff's voice.

"'All my life, sir,' he said. That poor clerk offered to lead him upstairs to his room, and Mr Reiff let him."

Just then someone called out Fanny's name. "Fanny, Fanny," it was Mr Murray's voice calling her and Fanny turned toward him. "I want to read you something from today's newspaper. A reporter has written about the poem you gave last evening. Here, it says, 'There was a touching piece of poetry, the composition of one of the sightless young ladies, and recited by herself in a modest and yet distinct manner, that could not have failed to reach all but marble hearts.'"

"That reporter was very kind," Fanny said. She had been told that forty-seven blind children lived in the area, and the poem was about a blind child. "If only some of the parents will send their children to the Institute I'll be happy," she added. She did not know that on the last part of the trip one very special student would be enrolled. His name was Alexander Van Alstyne and he was legally blind. His mother promised to bring him to the Institute, begging Fanny to "please look after him."

Like Fanny, Van as she called him, loved music. But Fanny didn't know then what part Van would play in her life.

One cold winter's day Fanny heard a frantic voice urging her out of her slumber. "Fanny, Fanny, you must get up." It was Anna's voice; her hand shaking Fanny's shoulder. Fanny pulled the covers up closer to her chin and kept her eyes shut. The trip home had left them all worn out and Fanny felt a tiredness that lasted into the winter. January cold seeped into the dorm room, and all Fanny wanted to do was stay in her warm bed. This morning a determined Anna stood over her. "Please, let me help you get up and downstairs on time for breakfast," Anna pleaded. "You hardly eat these days and I'm worried about you," Anna persisted. "The trip to Washington DC is next week, and I'm afraid you won't be able to go."

Fanny pushed herself up in bed. "Oh Anna, what was I thinking. I must go to Washington. It's the chance of a lifetime to speak before the Congress of the United States. I have to go, and you're right if Dr Clements thinks I'm not well he won't allow me to go. A little cold water on my face and I'll be awake." Fifteen minutes later Fanny and Anna walked into the dining room. Fanny tried to eat more than she really wanted.

"Fanny must not go to Washington," Mr Murray said. He was seated across from Dr Clements in the superintendent's office. "I believe the girl is ill and ought to be sent home for a good rest."

Dr Clements fiddled with a paper on the desk in front of him. "Certainly, a vacation back home with her folks would do Miss Crosby good. But, this trip to Washington means everything to her. I believe she would be truly ill if we kept her from her dream of going there. I promise you that I shall watch her carefully and see to it that she gets her rest on the trip. My advice is that you let her go."

"Well," Mr Murray said slowly, "if it's your professional opinion that she may go, then let her go. We would certainly miss our star exhibit."

On the night of the performance before the Congress and the President of the United States, her throat felt dry and her hands cold. Fanny was patriotic from her toes up and here she was about to stand in front of the Congress!

When it was her turn she whispered a prayer and began the poem she had written just for this night. At the end there was a moment of silence, and then a thunderous applause that startled Fanny. "Another, another, was the cry."

Dr Clements whispered, "I don't know, Fanny, if you should tax your strength anymore tonight, child."

"I think I have a shorter poem that I can use, if they wish me to," Fanny said. Dr Clements patted her shoulder, and Mr Murray led her back to the center of the platform where she stood, a slender, not very tall, young woman whose musical voice soon captured her audience. This time her poem was a tribute to one of the legislators who had recently died. When she finished Mr Murray wiped away his own tears as he led her back to her seat.

"Now," Dr Clements insisted, "I am sending you home, Fanny, for a good rest." Fanny was glad to be going back home to her mother and the old familiar farmhouse. A few days later she arrived in Bridgeport where Grandfather was waiting for her with the wagon. "Your mother will be powerful glad to see you, Fanny," he said, lifting her in his strong arms onto the wagon seat. "And Julia and Caroline are bursting with the surprises they've planned for you. Terrible thing their pa did running off with the Mormons out west and leaving your mother with two little ones to care for. His own son hid out until he was sure his pa was gone. He's a fine boy that brother of yours, and a big help to your Mother and me."

Fanny shook her head. "I was so sorry to hear that Mother's new husband left his own children behind and became a Mormon. Anyway, he's gone for good now, and I can't wait to hug my little sisters and that brother of mine."

When the time came to return to the Institute Fanny felt rested and well again. Though she was teaching full time, she managed to write well into the night. At last her dream of putting together a book of her poems was coming true. Whenever he could Dr Clements wrote down the poems she dictated from her memory. The book *The Blind Girl and Other Poems* was finished and published before the year of 1844 ended, the same year Fanny had her 24th birthday.

The school sold many copies, and kept it on display for visitors who might want to purchase one. One day Fanny was standing near the book display when a visitor asked if she knew anything about the author of the book. Instantly Fanny's love of a joke got the better of her.

"Yes, I know Miss Fanny Crosby, and I'm afraid she is not very agreeable at all," Fanny said. The visitor was sorry to hear that but bought the book anyway. As the visitor left, Fanny smiled at another prank well done. An hour later her heart sank when she learned that the visitor had been a famous professor at Columbia College. "When will I ever learn?" she said. "If only I'd known it was him. There was so much I could have asked him." She was determined to change her behavior, she must. Her prank had lost her a great opportunity. Fanny heard Lucy's soft voice calling her. It must be time for class. Fanny sighed. There was so much to do, and so little time it seemed. However, life was about to change for Fanny and everyone else at the Institute though not in the way any of them would have chosen.

Bring Out Your Coffins

These days Fanny and the others eagerly waited to hear the evening newspaper read to them. All of New York was anxiously listening for news of the terrible scourge of sickness that had already killed thousands in Europe. There was no known cure, and in Great Britain 70,000 had died adding to the thousands of dead in Persia and other countries. Now the disease was making its way across the ocean. A ship headed to New Orleans had buried seventeen passengers at sea all dead from cholera. From the port in New Orleans the disease spread inland. Soon St. Louis, Cincinnati, and Chicago followed with many dying from the epidemic. In May a ship landed in New York harbor with an ill passenger who died of the disease. By May 17th cholera had come to New York. "Would it sweep the city?" "Was the Institute in danger?" Like a sudden flood the epidemic spilled into New York leaving the dying and dead in its wake. Death struck from the poor in tenement buildings to the mansions of the rich. The newly elected president of the United States, President Polk, died of the disease. The mayor of New York City ordered all who could leave for the countryside to go. The Institute was closed and those students who could go home were instructed to do so. Fanny and others of the staff volunteered to stay and help.

Dr Clements stood watching a number of the staff and students who had volunteered to help him. "Yes, that's right," Dr Clements said. "You must be careful to see with your fingers that the level of opium in the spoon is exactly level and not one grain more. The calomel must be two level spoons—no more no less. There you go, mix them well, Fanny, that is exactly right and you know how to roll up each pill tightly. I am afraid we will need every pill you volunteers can make." Soon 500 to 800 in Manhattan were dead of cholera. In two months, 2,262 New Yorkers were dead. A hospital for cholera patients was opened nearby and then a school one block from the Institute was turned into a hospital. It was here that the sick from the Institute were taken, and where Fanny and the other volunteers worked night and day.

Fanny hurried down the hallway of the makeshift hospital to the next room where patients needed her help. Already ten of the students had died. The pills were no cure but the hope was they might help some. It was all they had to give. Fanny washed fevered faces and hands, bathed, prayed for, and sometimes sang softly to the dying of God's love. It was hard and she was worn out. She began to dread the daily call of the truckman, "Bring out your coffins." There were so many deaths. When someone came calling her to come quickly to little Lizzie's bedside, Fanny cried out. Stumbling in her haste she bumped into a new coffin sitting in the hallway outside the large room where patients lay in beds assembled in long rows.

The messenger who had come for Fanny led her to the side of the iron cot where, little Lizzie lay, one of Fanny's own pupils. Fanny found her small hand, hot and dry and lifted it to her cheek. "I'm here, Lizzie dear," she said as she sat on the side of the bed.

Like all her blind students, Lizzie let her fingers touch Fanny's face for a moment. Too weak to hold her arm up the fingers soon fell away. "Miss Crosby, I'm going home," Lizzie said in the small voice of a tired child. "Will you hold me, please?"

Fanny lifted the little one onto her lap and held her close. "Miss Crosby, I just wanted to say goodbye and tell you I love you. You can put me down now."

Fanny's tears rained down upon them both as she whispered back, "I love you too, Lizzie dearest." In moments Lizzie was gone home as she had said, and Fanny's heart was broken. That night Fanny felt feverish and ill. Was she coming down with the sickness too? Wearily she prayed for healing, swallowed several of the pills and went to bed. In the morning she awakened with no signs of the dread disease.

At last the mayor of New York declared that it was safe for folks who had left their homes to return to the city. The students were back and Fanny should have begun teaching but it was not to be.

Dr Clement's voice was kind but firm. "Fanny, I am sending you home to rest. You have nearly caught the disease yourself, and all the hours of nursing have left you completely worn out. I am ordering that you do not return until you are fully recovered. Drink plenty of milk and get some weight on you, child, and rest."

Fanny had never been so tired or felt so empty. Lucy helped her pack the few things she would need to take home with her. "I will be longing for you to come back well," Lucy said. "You must rest, and have someone write and let us know how you are."

"I will be glad to be home for awhile," Fanny said. "Lately with all this death and sorrow I've thought again and again of my grandmother's last question to me, and maybe going home I will have time to think about it."

Fanny was soon surrounded by her two younger sisters' joyous energy and her mother's strong determination that Fanny should get well. "Good food and plenty of fresh air and rest is what you need," she said. Fanny let them fuss over her. She was too tired to care. The days went by slowly it seemed to her, but at last her mother declared herself satisfied with Fanny's return to health. And Fanny did feel her old energy returning. What no one knew was the growing fear inside her that she could not answer her grandmother's question. She had never had what church folks called a conversion, a time when you knew with all your heart you had given your whole life to God. Many people wept when it happened. Fanny had not known such a time. She was as unsure she would go to heaven if she died, as she had been the day her grandmother asked her. Only now, since the terrible loss of little Lizzie and so many others, the question came back to her again and again.

"Oh Fanny it's good to have you back," Anna said hugging her close. "I prayed so hard, and wondered if you would ever come back."

"Here I am, Anna, and glad to be back. I can't say I will ever be the same as before. This summer has changed me, but at least it is behind us." There was nothing else she could say. It was impossible to express how she really felt. She had finished another book of poems, but it wasn't her best work, though it would be published. She had some fame as the 'Blind Poetess' but there was still something missing. Was she doing things God wanted her to do? Why didn't she feel sure and happy? What would Grandmother say to her if she saw her now? Fanny turned to teaching and doing all the things she had always done at the school, and soon was too busy to think about anything else. It didn't matter if she was happy or not, only that she was busy and tired enough at night to fall asleep quickly.

"Fanny, don't forget you promised to go with me to the revival meeting at the Broadway Tabernacle next Wednesday." The voice was Theodore Camp's, the industrial science teacher. Fanny loved his cheerfulness and they had become close friends. She promised to be ready for the meeting, but that night her old trouble came back.

Fanny dreamed that Theodore was dying, and she had been called to his bedside.

"Fanny, you must give up our friendship," he said.

"No!" Fanny cried. "You are my advisor, my friend. What will I do without your help?"

"I am longing to go home, Fanny, and I must. But will you meet me in heaven?"

Terror filled Fanny's heart. It was the same question her grandmother had asked her, and she had no different answer. "I hope so, with God's help," she said. Suddenly Fanny awoke and knew that it had all been a dream. But now the question was back, and Fanny could not forget it. Would she meet anyone she knew in heaven? "I'm a teacher now; I have the education I always dreamed of; I've published books of poetry, I play the piano in church when I'm asked, I know God is good and I do pray. I welcome visitors to the school and write poems for them, I have friends and a good family, what is missing?"

Wednesday evening came and Fanny sat by Theodore in a pew near the front. The sermon had been a powerful call to come to the Lord Jesus and afterward people went to the front and knelt down, some of them sobbing, others crying out while the church deacons and elders prayed for them. Fanny listened as several people rose to their feet and testified that they were saved! Many seemed overcome with their new joy. As Theodore and Fanny left the church, Fanny decided she would come again. The revival meetings were planned to go on through the fall.

"You poor thing," Anna whispered. They had gone together to the meetings and each time Fanny had gone to the front, knelt, and hoped for that thing called 'a conversion' to happen to her. Twice the elders had prayed over her but she'd felt no sudden feeling of great joy the way she thought it was supposed to come. For a third time Fanny went forward. No one else had gone forward this night. For two hours Fanny knelt there while the elders prayed for her in loud voices. Nothing happened. The congregation began to sing a hymn by Isaac Watts, one that Fanny knew well. On the last verse as they sang the words, "Here, Lord, I give myself away. Tis all that I can do" something did happen, something wonderful.

Like light breaking into her heart and flooding over her, Fanny knew that at last she saw what the Lord was saying to her all along. She had never really given everything over to the Lord, all of her life. "For the first time I realized that I had been trying to hold the world in one hand and the Lord in the other," she said later. Forgetting everyone around her and filled with all her old warmth and energy, Fanny stood up and sang "Hallelujah."

Anna and Theodore were as excited as Fanny. "You will have plenty of ups and downs in life," Theodore said, "but you know your life belongs to the Lord and his plans for you are good."

"Oh, Fanny, Theodore is right. We don't grow up overnight but the Lord Jesus will be there to care for us and help us, and I know how shy you are to even think about giving your testimony in church. It will happen, Fanny, you'll see."

"Only pray for me," Fanny said, "that when I do speak I won't have self-pride doing it. I've lived so long to make myself a success and falling into pride has been so easy for me." She remembered now the time Mr Jones had pointed out her pride in her early student days.

Fanny did give her testimony a week later at a church class meeting where she also played the piano for the singing. She found her words came slowly at first, and then joyfully as she told the truth of how the missing part of her life had suddenly become clear. She knew she truly belonged to the Lord in a new way, and there was no doubt that one day she would see her dear grandmother again.

Time passed quickly as Fanny gave herself to teaching, writing, church meetings, and greeting distinguished visitors. "It will be good to get away," she said to Anna as they packed for a short summer vacation. "Mother is happy that I'm bringing home friends from the Institute. Ted and Jack are looking forward to a week in the countryside, and I know you and Mary will love it too." I should warn you that my two little sisters are convinced their big sister is the greatest poet ever and they'll want to hear everything new I've written."

Anna smoothed a final handkerchief into place. "Just thinking of getting away for walks and talks and no school work at all makes me feel like I'm ready for anything."

Before too long the travelers were off on their vacation. The coach ride jostled over a rough road badly in need of repair. Seated across from Fanny and the girls, Jack groaned. "Sorry," he said. "It's this headache. I woke up this morning with it and can't seem to shake it."

"There's nothing worse for a headache than this kind of constant jolting," Fanny said, "but when we arrive my mother may have just the right kind of tea for you. She's very good at that kind of thing." But it wasn't tea Fanny's mother had in mind.

After they had eaten a hearty meal of country fresh bread, new potatoes and onions, roasted chicken and green beans, and rhubarb strawberry cobbler Fanny's mother went to fetch what she called her "sure" headache cure.

Setting a bowl full of salt next to Jack's place her Mother dipped her hands into the salt and said. "Now young man, this is a bit messy, but I assure you it will work. I'll just rub a good bit of this salt into your scalp and soon you will feel better."

"No, no thanks, I mean. Please you mustn't," Jack said. Blind like Fanny and the others he raised his hands to where her mother's voice told him she must be standing, but Fanny's mother was not to be stopped.

With both hands full of salt she began to rub Jack's head. "You'll see, it won't hurt a…" her voice suddenly died away. "Oh, my," she said. "I did not know, oh my." Jack's hair had slid sideways and now hung halfway to his shoulder."

"Yes," Jack said quietly. "I should have told you right away. It's a wig. I have worn it ever since I lost all my hair many years ago."

"Oh dear," Fanny's mother exclaimed. "The salt rub won't help your hair roots at all, I fear." Fanny could hear her mother's embarrassment.

"Now, Jack," Fanny said, "Since none of us at school have ever seen you with or without your wig, it doesn't make any difference to us. But I bet you dreaded having salt all over it, just as I would. Mother, I told Jack you might have a tea for him, one to drink not to wear!" Fanny couldn't help laughing and thankfully Jack couldn't either. It was a week of laughter and good times and over all too soon.

On the morning they were to leave Fanny slipped away from the others to the little room where her grandmother used to sit in her old rocking chair with Fanny at her side. "Grandmother, I know you aren't here, but I just wanted to say, yes, yes, Grandmother dear, I will see you in heaven. Jesus has saved me too, and Grandmother I know now he has a place for me in heaven." Tears streamed down her face, but they were tears of joy. At last she knew her grandmother's faith was her own.

A Love Song

The school had a new literature teacher, William Cleveland, and a new secretary, his younger brother Grover. When their father died suddenly, William asked Fanny to talk to Grover, who was taking the death hard. Grover was sixteen years-old, a tall, thin, shy boy who spoke little, but Fanny soon won him over. One day Grover said, "Miss Crosby, if you need someone to write down your poems for you, I'd sure be glad to do it."

"That would be a wonderful help," Fanny said, and soon the two were sharing Fanny's writings and becoming friends. Neither of them dreamed that Grover Cleveland would one day become the 22nd president of the United States and a life-long friend of Fanny's.

Mr George Root had been a music instructor at the Institute, and though he had left the school, Fanny loved hearing how well-known he was becoming for his own music. She was surprised to meet him again at her new summer job teaching music at a music school in North Reading. "Fanny Crosby," Mr Root greeted her when they met, "you are the very person I've been looking for. I know your work, and if you are willing you are just the one I'm needing to write the words for some of my music."

"Willing?" Fanny laughed. "If there is something I'd rather do than work with you on some songs this summer, I can't think what it might be." Summer turned into fall, and then winter, and spring and summer again while Fanny wrote song after song for George Root's music. Their songs became hit songs like "Hazel Dell" about a black man mourning his lost love Nelly. Another, "Prairie Flower" was a song about a girl named Rosalie, and one that quartets loved to sing was "There's Music in the Air." Soon Fanny and George had produced more than sixty popular songs being sung all over the country. They also wrote musicals, large cantatas like *The Flower Queen*, the first written by an American. George gave Fanny an idea of what he wanted, sometimes hummed a bit of music or played a piece and Fanny would return the next day with the songs he needed. Together they wrote the songs and music for two more famous cantatas, *Daniel*, and *The Pilgrim Fathers*. Their music was used over and over as schools performed the works. As was the custom Fanny received one dollar, sometimes two, per song. The poems then became the property of the publisher, who of course made far more. Still teaching at the Institute, Fanny had no thought of even asking for more than the usual fee.

"Fanny, my class is learning the music from *The Flower Queen*," Anna told Fanny one afternoon. "It is so uplifting and at the same time the story keeps their interest."

"I'm so glad, Anna," Fanny said. "I think the Lord is pleased with whatever good things are in the songs. They are reaching a lot of students, I hear." They were passing the new superintendent's office when Fanny stood still and grasped Anna's arm. A loud angry voice was coming through the closed door.

"I will not tolerate lateness in a student in my school. You were reported late to your first class this morning, a full five minutes, sir. I will not hear an excuse. The rod will teach you to be on time, sir."

"Please no, Mr Cooper, sir. I forgot my book and went to get it, and that's what made me late. It won't happen again, I promise." Fanny didn't recognize the boy's voice.

"Silence," Mr Cooper roared. "Instead of five I shall count seven with my rod, two extra to remind you to take care to bring your book next time." Fanny shrank against Anna at the awful sound of the stick falling upon the boy who instantly cried out.

Anna pulled Fanny away and hurried her down the hall to the garden door. "I cannot stand the way Mr Cooper is running this school. He uses that stick to discipline the smallest of faults. I'm glad I will not be returning after this term is over."

Fanny brushed tears from her face. "Oh Anna, there is nothing we can do about him. He is a close friend of some of the board of managers. If the school ever lost its funding over a scandal, it would be worse for the whole blind community. I hate his ways, but our students are learning and they will graduate in spite of him."

"True, but Lucy and Mary have already resigned and found other jobs. How many others will leave before the board wakes up?"

The sound of music, a beautiful classical song came from one of the parlors, and Fanny lifted her head to listen. "That's Van playing. I always know when it's him. Hear the way he holds that little melody with one hand while the other plays all around it?"

"He's a great pianist," Anna said. "And from the reviews Dr Clements read to us in last evening's news, it seems he is also one of the finest organists in New York City, and still such a young man."

"Yes, it's true," Fanny agreed. Van was ten years younger than she but somehow he seemed older than his years. "He does live for his music and loves to teach it as well as perform it."

Anna gently patted Fanny's arm. "You, Fanny, can't say Van's name without your voice going all dreamy. As your best friend I can tell you what I think, and that's the two of you have a lot in common, and I don't mean just your music. Jack told me Van talks of little else these days but Fanny's poetry, Fanny's sweet singing voice, Fanny's fine music, Fanny's wise words, her teaching, and who knows what else!" Anna laughed lightly.

Fanny felt her face warming. "Hush Anna, you are just teasing me because you know I do think he is a fine young man in so many ways."

"Mark my words, Fanny. You might have to start listening to what your heart is saying. You are plainly in love with Van Alstyne. So please excuse me if I leave you right here at the parlor door where Mr Alstyne is performing. Catch you at supper," Anna called as Fanny heard her footsteps hurrying away.

Fanny stood in the hall and listened as Van continued playing. How long she stood there she didn't know. He had finished and Fanny was about to move on when Van called to her from the parlor. "Fanny, is that you?"

Fanny turned back toward the doorway where his voice had come from. "Yes, but how did you know?"

Van laughed. "I thought I heard Anna's voice calling 'Catch you at supper,' and hoped it was you she meant. Do you have time for a walk in the garden?"

"I'd love it," Fanny said. She knew where Van was leading them as they turned the garden path near the fragrant crocuses that had come up early this year. Van chose a bench nested against a large tulip tree. Though the March sun was warm it was still a bit cool and Fanny drew her shawl close as she sat down next to Van.

"Let me warm those small hands of yours," Van said taking hers in his own. "Besides I have something to say, Fanny, and I need to know what you think of it." Like most of the blind, both could often tell more by the shake of a hand than a sighted person might. He would know if Fanny quickly withdrew her hands that she was not ready for what he had to say. "I was gone over the weekend as you know," he said, "but what you don't know is that I was house hunting." He felt a small flutter move Fanny's hands. "Fanny, you must know that I love you and I want to marry you. Two of my sighted friends from church went with me to Maspeth, Long Island where one of them grew up. It's a wonderful quiet town in the countryside, and Fanny we found the perfect little house, one we can rent right away." Van was so excited he didn't stop long enough for Fanny to say a word. "You will have to give up your teaching at the Institute, but you've talked about doing that ever since Mr Cooper came and things here have changed. You can write while I play the organ in churches and give lessons, and with what I've already set aside it will be enough to meet our needs. You will love the house, Fanny." Van proceeded to describe it in detail.

Fanny laughed and gently removed one hand to grasp Van's arm. "Van, you haven't given me a chance to say what I can hardly wait to say. Yes, yes, dear heart, I do love you and I will marry you. I think God's loving hand surely has brought us together. There I've said it, and now you must tell me everything, when we shall be married, where, all the wonderful details." Three days later they were married. The little house was everything Fanny could have dreamed of.

Months passed keeping the house, tending the garden, doing all the chores Fanny had learned as a young girl at her grandmother's side. She didn't mind the young woman who came regularly to help with the few things she needed done. Evenings were wonderful as Van played his music and Fanny sang. Van liked classical music and Fanny soon learned to compose words for him. Fanny's mother visited them and when she left, Fanny was sure. She would tell Van that very evening; they were going to have a baby!

Fanny's heart sang day after day as she and Van waited for their precious little one. Fanny sewed and knitted until there was quite a pile of tiny clothes and things ready for this baby. She thought and thought about how they would bring up this child to learn all that a good education could teach him or her, including the wonderful sounds of a piano, a guitar, a harp, and eventually the organ. After all, this little one's father was not only a fine pianist; he was one of the finest organ players in New York. Her heart sang songs so happy she imagined them filling the rooms as she worked, notes of joy floating everywhere. "It won't be long, now," she whispered to herself as the time drew near.

A Deep Sorrow

Fanny sobbed until there were no more tears. The baby she had waited for, loved and held in her arms for such a short time, was gone. "When I held her tiny body close, I imagined all the years ahead we would have to love her as she grew," Fanny said. "But we never had a chance. No day goes by when I don't think of her." Her words ended with a sob. Seated next to her on the couch, Anna wrapped her tightly in her arms.

Two months ago Fanny's friend, Anna, had come to the funeral for Fanny's weeks-old infant. The baby had died in her sleep. Both Van and Fanny had sorrowed deeply, but though Van had gone back to his teaching and playing, Fanny was still mourning heavily. Worried for her friend, Anna visited as often as she could. This morning she had found Fanny weeping. Anna put her arms around Fanny's shaking shoulders. "Dear heart," she said, "all we can say is that she is with Jesus now." Fanny continued to cry as Anna rubbed her back. "Do you remember the poem you wrote to your Mother when your tiny infant sister died while we were at school?" she asked. Fanny nodded. "You meant every word you wrote then, Fanny, when you said she was with the Lord Jesus. If you can think of your little sister and your daughter together now with the dear Lord, it may comfort you too." Anna prayed silently that Fanny would find comfort. "You will always miss her," Anna said as tears ran down her own face. "I can only pray that in time this terrible wound in your heart will begin to heal, dearest."

Fanny was sure she would never heal. Every room in the little house brought back her grief. Van was busier than ever, and often gone from home because of his work, but even he could tell that living in their quiet little house was not doing them good. "Fanny, it's time we moved," Van said, "back to the city where there is more for you to do, and less travel for me." And so began the first of many moves.

Near the Institute they found rooms in a house that rented to the blind. Van and Fanny were the only married couple there. For a while this was a good location for Van's work as well as Fanny's. The cantatas Fanny and Root had written together were becoming popular, especially *The Flower Queen*. Fanny was invited to many of the performances. It was now thought of as America's first opera-like musical. She also took some invitations to play the harp, a skill she had learned at the Institute. Sometimes Van would compose a piece of music for Fanny to write the words to. "Ah, Fanny, you and Van write such beautiful songs together," visiting friends would say, "and they are so complex, so different from the common hymns we hear," many added. But as Fanny would discover, the songs were not the kind people could remember, not the kind of songs publishers wanted for hymnals.

Songs like "They Have Sold Me Down the River," were popular. Anti-slavery feelings were in the air in New York and Fanny and Mr Root were strongly against slavery. As the war between the North and South approached, Fanny's patriotism grew along with her songs supporting the North.

One summer day Fanny met a friend for lunch at a restaurant near the heart of the city's shopping center. Fanny pinned the small silk Union flag she liked to wear, to the front of her dress. When Fanny and her friend were seated at a table, a woman, who supported the south, loudly demanded, "Take that dirty rag away. Yes, I mean that union flag pin you dare to wear in public."

Fanny was on her feet instantly. "Take back those words," Fanny said. The young waiter who hurried to stand between them, fearing they would come to blows, tried to make peace. Fanny felt her face burning for her quick tempered words. Her friend took Fanny's arm and firmly suggested it was best that they leave.

Fanny's anger had already cooled as they walked down the street away from the restaurant. "My dear Fanny, you are so patriotic, that I feared for you. From the look on that woman's face I could see that she was a fanatical supporter of the South," her friend said. "I'm afraid that here in New York there are a number of people like that woman, though how anyone could be for slavery I do not understand."

"Yes, but I should never have lost my temper. I'm so sorry," Fanny said. "I know there is a better way, but I doubt that woman would listen to anything anyone tried to tell her."

"I believe you're right," said her friend patting Fanny's arm, "But you must keep on writing your songs for those who will."

Fanny did go on writing. On one of her new songs she asked that her married name be put down as the composer. That night she told Van thinking he might be pleased. Fanny was mistaken. "We need to talk," he said. When she was seated at the table across from him Van began. "You are Fanny Crosby, the blind poetess, author of several books, writer of cantatas and popular songs that people love, and a skilled harpist. People come to your recitals to hear you play the harp because they know the name Fanny Crosby," Van said. "I must insist that you use your own name on all your works, and not the lesser-known married name of Fanny Alstyne." Surprised, Fanny started to rise, but Van reached for her hand and held it gently. "It's only wise, Fanny, to use the gift God has given you in the best possible way. And that brings me to tell you something else. I've been asked to teach at the music summer camp this year. However, I must stay on site for much of the time. I feel I have to do this my dear."

Fanny pressed Van's hand gently. "I understand, dearest," she said. "I am happy for you, Van, even though I've promised to work on more songs, and couldn't possibly go with you." Chuckling first, she mimicked Van's voice, "You must do everything you can do with your talents, it's only wise to use God's gift in the best way possible."

Van laughed. She had quoted his very words back to him. As Fanny turned to fix their supper, she hoped she had meant them. Their careers seemed to be taking them apart more and more. Fanny changed the subject, "I've got a chicken stewing and fresh bread for supper. Let's ask our two new neighbors to help us eat it. We can have an evening of music if they'll stay." Fanny loved sharing Van's piano playing with others, and enjoyed playing her guitar for a sing-a-long. Van sighed as he made his way to the door to invite the newly moved in neighbors. He had learned one sure thing about Fanny's nature. To share was a part of her, and putting aside special time for themselves wouldn't happen that often. Fanny gave away to the poorer folks around them whatever she and Van had to spare beyond their daily needs. He sighed again. At least tonight it was just their dinner.

It was not long before Van found them an apartment that would cost less and still meet their needs. The rent was cheaper in the new place so it also meant a poorer neighborhood. This didn't trouble Fanny, however. For Fanny the poorer tenements were just where she and Van could do some good. The neighborhood was racially mixed. Many of the neighbors were German and Irish immigrants who loved music. Fanny grew fond of her near neighbor, a black woman whose soft, cheerful voice went right to Fanny's heart. Mary Jackson's family was large and Fanny delighted in the children. Each time she visited Mary it seemed someone in the family was having a birthday, or celebrating a new tooth, or just bursting to share something with Fanny, who was always ready to join in. When Fanny learned that the children listened to her play her guitar each night, she invited them all for an evening of song. Others soon crowded into the small apartment, and Fanny loved it. Van who had a heart for teaching poor children to play, offered to teach one of the older children, a quiet lad but eager to learn.

Life in a New York City tenement meant noise, no running water, hallways that filled with the smells of cooking of all kinds, no indoor plumbing just privies in the courtyard. Living close to one's neighbors also meant sometimes sharing in the sorrows and hardships of the poor and working class. Fanny's blindness made her the object of the neighbor children's special interest. She loved hearing them call to her in the hallways, "Miss Fanny, you want a hand up them stairs?" And she always did, letting them carry a package or open a door, knowing that they were probably hungry for the treat they knew she would have for them. Her grandmother had taught Fanny how to bake bread and many other things, so that Fanny often took a loaf where there was sickness or trouble. Fanny didn't mind the rickety stairs or the tenement smells, she just loved doing what she could to help others.

She also attended the sewing circles at the John Street Methodist Church to sew and knit for the poor. From childhood Fanny had learned to do both well and loved to keep her hands busy making little gifts, meeting needs where she could. Though deep inside her she would always carry a sweet sorrow, her heart could sing again and her hands could do the things she loved.

In spite of the growing threat of conflict between the North and the South, something great and good was happening all over New York City, and Fanny couldn't help being a part of it. Churches everywhere were growing, and at John Street crowds of 1200 filled the church at its noon-time prayer meetings as people began to see the need for God in their lives. Sunday schools were bursting, the YMCA work to reach young men with the good news of Jesus had begun in the cities, missions to reach the down and out were thriving, along with vast revival meetings. It was being called a new Awakening after the First Great Awakening back in the 1740s. But soon all attention was turned to the terrible announcement of war! The shadow of war that had hung over the country was no longer a mere threat. In April of 1861, war between the North and the South was declared.

Like those standing near her, Fanny wept openly on the day the newsboys on every New York City corner cried the headlines, "War declared! President Lincoln calls every able-bodied man to defend the nation." It would be a long and terrible war. Fanny hurried down the street to the corner where the horse-drawn omnibus she needed would stop. Her thoughts were on her family, surely her step-brother Will would be off to the war before the week was out. There were others too, cousins, that would join the army. She thought of the young men who had come to know the Lord during the last few months of meetings here in the city, and how many of them might soon be off to war. "Lord, help me to encourage them in every way I can," she prayed. She would pray for victory for the Union, the freeing of the slaves, and that peace would come soon.

Already as she listened for the bus to come, a song was forming in her mind, a song that spoke of courage, and right, and victory over the South. Unlike her other songs this one was fully patriotic and included no mercy for the enemy, the South that had once been a friend. In the months that followed, Fanny wrote war songs, but there was something missing in them. Words written to taunt the South's leader, Jefferson Davis and his troops, like:

> Death to those whose impious hands
> Burst our Union's sacred bands,
> Vengeance thunders, right demands
> Justice for the brave.

At the end of the song Jefferson is threatened with beheading. These were not Fanny's best work, and did not come from the song in her heart.

She Would Write Hymns!

Thanks to the telegraph news of the war traveled quickly. Fanny's hope for a quick victory faded as battles between the northern Union troops and the southern Confederate troops piled up deaths and destruction. The churches in New York City were soon doing what they could to help with the war effort. Fanny and two of her friends went together to the noontime prayer meetings at John's Chapel to pray for the troops, for President Lincoln and the country. The news from battles like Fredricksburg where 12,600 Union men died and many others were wounded was terrible. Churches began providing meals on special days to the wounded soldiers and their families to help with the needs. Bitter cold weather brought more suffering to the troops. Some reports said, "For every soldier killed in battle, two more dies of sickness in the winter camps." When the call went out for volunteers to knit 5,000 mittens desperately needed for the troops, Fanny spent all the time she could spare to help with the knitting.

Van was busier than ever as a church organist, music teacher, and much needed pianist for the many benefits held for the war effort. Van's fine musical talents had brought him friends among the wealthy who opened their homes to him, and he was frequently gone at the request of one or another. "Fanny, my dear," one of Van's friends said, "if only you could see Van's face when he plays, it is lit with joy, lost in the realms of music few of us may reach." Fanny nodded, sure that it must be so. Besides that, Van was usually the life of any gathering. He had a deep interest in people, and was welcome in society for his fine social skills as well as his musical talents. The demands of their careers took them away often. When close well-to-do friends provided Van a studio and a place to live in their home while he came and went, practiced and taught, Fanny agreed it was a good thing.

"God has given you great talents, Van. We're no longer so young, and it does me good to think you will have a fine studio and be free to pursue your music. I will be happy with a little place near to my work, and lots of quiet time to pray and think my songs. I will be your chief champion always, as you are for me, dear one, and come as often as I can."

Fanny moved into an apartment on the top floor of a tenement that was just right for her needs. Some of the landlords kept up their buildings, some didn't, leaving their tenants to live in poorly built, overcrowded, filthy apartments. It didn't take Fanny long to get acquainted with her new neighbors and she still kept in touch with the Jacksons and others from her old neighborhood. Most of these people were hard-working families with enough children to make her feel right at home. She smiled as her fingers wandered over her guitar strings. Soon she would invite her new neighbors for an evening of song.

On Sunday morning she could hear the church bells ringing everywhere. This morning she planned to go to the Dutch Reformed Church on 23rd Street. She visited there often. Reverend Peter Stryker was a fine preacher, and a friend she'd known from her days at the Institute.

After the service Reverend Stryker asked Fanny to stay a moment, he had something he hoped she could help him with. Finally the last of the congregation was leaving and the pastor returned to where Fanny stood waiting. He took her arm and led her into his office. When she was seated Reverend Stryker, said, "Fanny there are two things I wanted to talk to you about. First, our New Year's service is tomorrow night, and though I know this is short notice, I wonder if you could give us a poem as part of our program?" He waited while Fanny thought about his request.

"Yes, pastor, I believe I could do that, and I'd love to really," Fanny said.

"That's great, Fanny. I know God has gifted you as a poet, and lately I've heard some of the songs you wrote for Mr Root for the *Daniel* cantata. Very fine, indeed. That brings me to my second request." Pastor Stryker, paused, bowed his head for a moment and said. "Fanny we've known each other ever since you first visited here while you were still at the Institute. And if I may speak of it, Fanny, for a moment, I know that when you and Van moved back to the city after your child died, you've been doing many different things, war songs and the like, and I've wondered if you've found anything really satisfying for that talent of yours? I believe I have something that may interest you greatly." Fanny leaned forward in her chair. She felt as though Pastor Stryker was reading her mind. Fanny had been wondering what she might do next.

"Fanny, you are familiar with Mr William Bradbury and all his great work as a musician setting some of our famous old hymns into music for today." Fanny could only nod, she did know and admired Mr Bradbury very much. "Well, my dear, it seems that Mr Bradbury is anxious to find someone who can write new hymns for today. You are the very first, and only one who came to my mind. He would very much like to meet with you. What do you think, Fanny?"

"Oh, my, you can't imagine how I would like to meet with him," Fanny replied. She left the pastor's office feeling as if she could almost fly her heart was soaring so high.

"Don't forget our New Year's Eve poem," Reverend Stryker called out.

Fanny didn't forget, and that night with new hope she wrote a poem called "The Old Year". One stanza read:

> Thou art gone, and in thy place,
> With a bright and smiling face,

> Comes the New Year, fair as thou,
> With a chaplet[1] on his brow,
> And his voice is sweet and clear;
> Shall I weep for thee, Old Year?

Fanny's answer was no. The New Year held new hope for her, perhaps work with Mr Bradbury. That night Fanny dreamed, and in her dream, though she had never seen anything but the faintest of light, she could see everything in her dream plainly.

She dreamed she was being guided past the stars toward one shining brightly above a beautiful heavenly land. When they came to a river they stopped, and Fanny's guide told her she could not cross now, but must return to earth to do her work there. "But," her guide said, "before you go back, I will open the gates a little so you can hear one burst of heaven's music." What Fanny heard then in her dream she could only describe as melody such as she had never known existed, and afterwards thrilled to remember. She awakened, certain that God was truly assuring her that she should use her talents for the writing of hymns.

It was soon the time for Fanny to meet with Mr Bradbury at his office. He was based at the Ponton Hotel on Broome Street. Though she could not see him she had heard him described as a thin man with a small face surrounded by a great thicket of dark hair, and a large beard. She heard in his greeting more than what

---

[1] A circular wreath or garland.

most sighted people could ever hear, and she liked him at once. "Fanny," he said, "I thank God that we have at last met, for I think you can write hymns, and I have wished for a long time to have a talk with you." He immediately introduced her to his assistant, and Fanny's joy was complete! His assistant was none other than her old childhood friend, Vet (Sylvester) Main.

"Vet has become a well-known soloist in many New York churches, and a fine churchman in the Norfolk Street Methodist Church," Mr Bradbury said. In minutes Vet and Fanny were talking like the old friends they had been. When Fanny left it was with her first assignment: to write a hymn for Mr Bradbury.

Fanny began to run some words over her tongue. 'I think I've got the beginnings of a hymn,' she muttered. And she was right:

> We are going, we are going
> To a home beyond the skies,
> Where the fields are robed in beauty
> And the sunlight never dies.

Mr Bradbury at once chose it for his new hymnal and changed its name to "Our Bright Home Above".

The following week, Fanny was asked to write a war song for a secular publication Mr Bradbury was also doing. He suggested a first line, "There's a sound among the mulberry trees," only Fanny disliked it and offered, "There's a sound among the forest trees." Mr Bradbury liked that better too and played the music to accompany it. The piece was a difficult one. However, the following day Fanny came back with the finished song, a war hymn and presented it to Mr Bradbury's secretary who immediately sat down and played it through. He was astounded.

"Miss Crosby, no one ever thought you or anyone else could write words to that melody!" Mr Bradbury had given Fanny a near impossible task to test her, and she passed with excellence.

When Mr Bradbury heard the hymn for himself, he could only say, "Fanny, I'm surprised! And now, let me say, that while I have a publishing house you will always have work here at the William B. Bradbury firm."

Fanny went to work writing songs for Mr Bradbury right away. For each song or poem, she was paid $1.00, sometimes $2.00. For the rest of her life the pay remained the same. Once a song left Fanny's hands it became the property of the publisher and all future profits went only to the publishers. This was true for all song writers of the day, and Fanny was quite content with her pay. She loved writing hymns, many of them for the Sunday School hymnals Bradbury published. Her grateful heart was full now with the certainty that this was the Lord's will for her. It was with joy that she asked for God's blessing before she wrote each hymn.

When the news came in April, that her beloved president Lincoln had been assassinated, Fanny who had met him, and thought of him as one of the greatest men she had known, wept. She would always remember April, 1865, the date of his death as a night of deepest gloom.

The Civil War was over, and Fanny was busier than ever writing hymns for Bradbury. Most often Mr Bradbury played the music he wanted her to write for, but sometimes she was asked to make the poem before there was music for it. At times she got to choose her own topic and these could come from most anywhere. One day as Vet Main, Bradbury and the famous musician and singer Philip Phillips were talking with Fanny, Phillips declared he needed to leave. "Good night," he said, "until we meet in the morning." Fanny couldn't forget the words, and soon wrote a funeral hymn that began:

> Goodnight! Goodnight! Till we meet in the morning,
> Far above this fleeting shore;
> To endless joy in a moment awaking,
> There we'll sleep no more.

By April 1866, Mr Bradbury knew that he had only a short time to live. While he lay ill Fanny worked on the hymnals at the office. Her name was now well-known in the field of hymn writing, and Fanny was asked to write for other publishers of church music too. Fanny soon came to know one of them, Phoebe Palmer Knapp, very well. In fact Phoebe became a close friend of Fanny's. Phoebe was married to a wealthy businessman and would host famous musical events at the Knapp mansion. When Fanny first visited Phoebe's music salon Phoebe had led her through her collection of instruments. Fanny marveled at how many there were. "I do like to compose as well as sing," Phoebe told her. Fanny soon learned that though Phoebe didn't excel in either, none of her guests would ever tell her so.

Phoebe supported many charities, and would have added poor Fanny to the list had Fanny let her. "Not a thing do I need," Fanny said.

"At least I may count on you to write poems for me now and then, and my brother shall publish them at his own company," Phoebe insisted.

"That I would love to do," Fanny promised. And that very afternoon Phoebe played a piece for her that she had just composed. As Fanny listened the melody found its way into her heart and words began to form around it.

"Now, Fanny, what does my music say to you?" Phoebe asked.

"Why, it said, blessed assurance Jesus is mine," Fanny replied. And as the two sat there Fanny dictated the whole of the new hymn that had come to her through Phoebe's music.

All too soon the news Fanny had been dreading came. Mr Bradbury was dying, and he had called for Fanny. As she stood at his bedside he said, "I am going to be forever with the Lord; and I will await you on the bank of the river."

Fanny wept. "Oh, must I lose a friendship that I have enjoyed so much?" she said.

"No," Mr Bradbury replied in a faint voice. "Take up my lifework where I lay it down; and you will not lose a friendship, though I am going away. You will strengthen it by carrying out my work."

At his funeral, Fanny heard someone say, "Fanny pick up the work where Mr Bradbury leaves it, and dry your tears." Fanny never knew who said the words but she knew she must follow them.

After Mr Bradbury's death the company name was changed to Biglow and Main. Fanny was soon contributing to the new hymnal *Song Book of Bright Jewels*, especially published for the Sunday School market. One morning, her old friend, Vet had come in to work while Fanny dictated a new song to a secretary.

"Fanny," Vet called out, "Listen to this! It's hard to believe that the last three hymn books have sold over 1.7 million copies. Fanny clapped her hands for joy. "And," Vet went on, "your songs are being sung all over the country in Sunday Schools everywhere. It does my heart good," he said, "to think that Sunday School libraries are stocked with good children's stories and songs. In small towns they are the only libraries for children."Vet went quickly to the piano and began playing one of Fanny's children's songs. "This is one of my favorites, Fanny, sing it with me." Fanny's sweet soprano sang along with Vet's deep voice:

> *There's a city that looks o'er the valley of death,*
> *And its glories may never be told.*
> *There the sun never sets, and the leaves never fade*
> *In that beautiful city of gold.*

"Fanny, it's a song of hope for thousands of children," Vet said quietly as they finished.

Help me Speak to Them

In her small attic apartment Fanny prepared herself to work on a new hymn. It seemed quieter here than in the old tenement where Mary Laverpool, and Jacob the shoemaker, young Isaac the black porter, and Jacko the grocer had been her neighbors. She thought of the evenings they'd come together to sing songs. Did they still sing her songs. She'd heard dear Mary singing them many times through the thin tenement walls. "I just loves singing about Jesus," Mary had told her. "Yore songs, they is so easy to remember a body can sing them anywheres." Fanny smiled. She'd written one called "I Love the Name of Jesus" while Mr Bradbury was still alive. "May the songs always be about you, Lord. And easy to remember," she added

Fanny left her tenement each day, walked the city blocks now firmly mapped in her mind, listening all the while to the sounds of wagons, coaches, vendors, children, and the occasional greeting of neighbors' familiar voices as she passed. The children who knew her would sometimes walk with her to the corner, and Fanny loved their company. She wore her dark glasses, the usual sign of a blind person and often a policeman or some kind passerby offered assistance when she needed it. She managed quite well traveling the city on her own. Only once she did somehow step on a conductor's foot as she climbed onto the bus. "Oh, I am so sorry," she had said, but the conductor was kind and saw to it that she soon had a seat.

She loved going to work at the music publishing firm, and since Mr Bradbury's death Fanny now did most of the selecting of tunes and set the style for the hymns published.

A cold November wind blew gustily and Fanny drew her coat collar close as she hurried to the office. Her hands and feet were cold, but her heart was warm as she thought of her latest project with Philip Phillips. Their work on *The Triumph of the Cross* was finished. Philip's music was fine and she'd been pleased with the words she had written for it. Fanny thought she felt a snowflake! It made her think of Christmas and home with the family in Bridgeport. This year she might even take up her little nephew John's invitation to go sledding with him. She laughed as she opened the office door and warm air greeted her.

"Ah, Fanny," Philip said, "I shall be meeting the famous Mr Howard Doane at the Pontoon Hotel where he is staying. He has asked to see the new cantata. He is a wealthy man who has a love for music and writes well, but he is the first to admit that he lacks the ability to fit suitable words to his works. Poor fellow, if only he had a Fanny Crosby he should do well."

Fanny laughed. She had never met Mr Doane. The day passed quickly and that night Philip's words came back to her. She ate a light meal of bread and sausage and afterwards sat thinking about a hymn that had been trying to find its way into her mind for awhile now. As always she prayed, and then began to compose the words coming to her again into a poem. Finally, it was finished and Fanny slept at last tired but happy. In the morning the name Mr Doane came to her mind. The same thing happened after her morning prayer. Fanny wondered, and then she smiled. "Lord, do you think Mr Doane would like to see the hymn I wrote last night?" Her answer came so quickly she smiled again, as the word of a well-known Bible verse came to her mind: "Take every opportunity to do good."

"Ah, surely it would be a kindness to send it to him," she said. First she must dictate it to her secretary at work, and after that send it to Mr Doane at his hotel.

As Fanny left her apartment, the washerwoman's son John greeted her from the hallway. "John, are you free today to take a message for me? I shall pay you for your trouble," she said. "You will have to go with me to my office and wait while I have the message written down. Are you familiar with the Pontoon Hotel?'

Downtown in his hotel room, Mr Doane put his briefcase on the dresser. He didn't bother to open it. There was nothing in it he could use this time. Poor Van Meter his friend was doing his best at the Five Points Mission to make the anniversary of the mission in two days an event that would touch the hearts of his people. "I've failed him, Lord," Doane whispered. "I can write the music he wants for a fine anniversary hymn but what good is it without meaningful words?" Doane knelt by his bed. "Lord I need a poem for this tune. In fact I'm asking for someone who can write poems so that we can have hymns and so that I can do the work you've given me to do, Lord." He'd barely finished praying when someone knocked on the door. A young rather ragged looking boy stood in the hallway with a message in his hand. Doane thanked him and gave the lad a nickel.

The message was from Fanny Crosby. It said: "Mr Doane: I have never met you, but I feel impelled to send you this hymn. May God bless it."

As Doane read the words tears streamed down his face; it was exactly what he needed for the Five Points Mission program.

> More like Jesus would I be
> Let my Savior dwell with me,
> Fill my soul with peace and love,
> Make me gentle as the dove;
> More like Jesus as I go,
> Pilgrim, in this world below;
> Poor in spirit would I be
> Let my Savior dwell in me.

Doane hurried back to the mission and practically dragged Van Meter to a nearby church where he could play the new hymn on the organ. Van Meter was supposed to pump the reed organ while Doane played and sang, but as he listened Van Meter forgot all about pumping. Instead he was weeping. Doane told Van Meter the whole story. "Now, my friend," he said, "you have the wonderful hymn you hoped for, and I must find Miss Fanny Crosby," Doane said.

It was not often that a well-dressed gentleman like Mr Doane climbed tenement stairs to knock at the door of an attic apartment. For sometime Doane had searched for Fanny Crosby and could only hope that this really was her address.

"How can she be living in such a poor run-down neighborhood as this?" Doane puzzled. In answer to his knock the door opened to reveal a very short woman, older than he expected but perhaps she could tell him if Miss Crosby lived here. When he asked the woman's reply left him astounded.

"I am Miss Crosby, and so glad to meet you, Mr Doane. Please do come in."

They talked and afterwards as Doane left he insisted on giving Fanny payment for her fine poem. Fanny thought it was two dollars he gave her so she took it and thanked him. On her next trip to the grocers however she learned that the two dollars was actually twenty.

Mr Doane and his wife soon became close friends of Fanny's, and it was Mr Doane who put over a thousand of Fanny's poems to music. The Doanes insisted that Fanny spend vacation time with them at their summer place. Fanny was especially grateful for one thing: Mr Doane's music was easy to remember when people heard it once or twice. The people Fanny hoped to reach with her songs didn't have pianos, were too poor to own hymnals, and the songs they heard in church really

115

needed to be the kind they could easily memorize. When Mr Doane called on Fanny one day to ask if she could write a poem using the phrase, "Pass Me Not, O Gentle Savior," Fanny said yes, but in the weeks that followed nothing came to her.

It was spring and Fanny was to speak at a prison in Manhattan. Her hymns were well-known and she was often asked to speak to groups like the YMCA, to churches, missions, and in prisons such as this one. As the chaplain and his two helpers walked with Fanny past the metal gates that clanged close behind them, Fanny felt the cold, dank air of the prison around her. In the room where the meeting was held, she listened to the sound of the prisoner's footsteps as they were led in. Some shuffled, others were heavy steps. "Help me to speak to them," Lord she prayed.

When Fanny was introduced, she felt the love and peace that filled her each time she spoke. She began as always, "I am so happy to be here with you this evening." Her words were simple, loving, reaching out to the men before her with the good news of Jesus. She told them stories of her childhood and then ended with a poem she'd written for them. When she sat down again and waited for the chaplain to end the meeting, Fanny heard one of the prisoners pleading, "Good Lord! Do not pass me by!" The sound of his heartfelt words stayed with her long after the prisoners were marched back to their cells. That night she wrote the hymn using Mr Doane's phrase:

> Pass me not, O gentle Savior,
> Hear my humble cry,
> While on others Thou art smiling,
> Do not pass me by.

The second verse too came to her:

> Savior, Savior,
> Hear my humble cry,
> While on others Thou art calling,
> Do not pass me by.

Mr Doane wrote the music and a few nights later the song was sung at the same prison where Fanny was speaking again. That very night some of the prisoners made the choice to turn their lives over to Jesus and confessed their faith in him before the others. Fanny never knew if the man she'd heard pleading with the Lord was one of them or not, but she was greatly overjoyed for the ones who had come to the Lord.

The next time Mr Doane appeared at Fanny's apartment he came with an urgent request. "Fanny I have only forty minutes before my train leaves for Cincinnati, and I have written a piece of music for you. If I hum it for you can you memorize it and write the words for it?" Fanny agreed and listened as he hummed.

As he finished Fanny said, "The music is saying, 'Safe in the arms of Jesus!' Wait here a few minutes." Fanny hurried into her bedroom, closed the door and prayed, as she always did, for help to write this hymn. A few minutes later she finished it and quickly dictated the poem to Doane who thanked her and hurried away. The song was published and would become one of her best loved, best known songs. Fanny's heart knew for certain that her own tiny infant was one of those truly "Safe in the arms of Jesus."

Fanny was visiting the Doanes when Mr Doane again asked her to write a hymn on something for home missions, and gave her the phrase "Rescue the Perishing." This time it was while Fanny was speaking to a group of working-men near the Doane's home that Fanny was again touched by the desperate need she sensed present in the meeting. She felt it so strongly that she stopped speaking to ask if some young man was there in urgent need of help, someone who had wandered from his home and his mother's teaching. "I would like to meet with you, after the service," she said. Fanny knew it was God's doing when a young man came to her at the close of the meeting.

He said to her, "Do you mean me? I promised my mother to meet her in heaven, but the way I've been living, I don't think that will be possible now."

"Nothing is impossible with God," Fanny said gently. That night the young man came to the Lord Jesus. When they had prayed together he left trusting the Lord, and sure that one day in heaven he would see his mother again. Fanny went home and that night wrote the hymn "Rescue the Perishing." The last line of the first verse said, "Tell them of Jesus the mighty to save." When it was published it too became one of the most loved hymns of mission workers everywhere. To tell of Jesus, the mighty to save, was the true song of her heart.

Mr Moody and Mr Sankey

Fanny had come to visit Van, and he had just asked her to do a concert with him. Fanny clapped her hands for joy! "Yes, yes, Van, let's do a concert and give everything we make to the poor. Van, you know I love listening to you play and these days I rarely get to hear the old masters that you bring so alive. I sometimes find myself humming one of your beautiful pieces. I truly do miss great music." Fanny sighed, "but I love what I do too. It's wonderful to see how many people are touched by the simple music of our hymns, especially those who only know popular music."

"Then you will play the harp, my dear, and we shall give a benefit[1] full of music for those who can pay for the tickets and come expecting fine music," Van said. "And then we shall give the proceeds to the poor." The night of the concert was packed, and Fanny's heart soared with the harp as she played. Afterwards her friend Mrs Knapp insisted Fanny and Van must play again for the small gatherings she loved to hold at the Knapp mansion.

By this time Fanny could no longer count the number of composers who wanted her poems for their

---

[1] A name given to a concert or performance that aims to raise money for charity.

music, or the number she wrote. Often she wrote more than one poem on a subject so that they could choose what worked best for them. Biglow and Main were one of the two biggest publishers of hymns, and Fanny would write for them alone 5,959 hymns. She wrote so many for their hymnals that she was now asked to use pen names so that no one book would be almost all just Fanny's songs. Fanny came up with 204 different pen names! Some like Sally Smith, Sam Smith, Victoria Sterling, Rian J. Sterling, Julia Sterling. Many of her names sounded pretty strange. She had always loved a good joke and still did. Fanny was busy, and soon to be even busier!

"Phoebe, I really want to hear Mr Moody and the singer Ira Sankey," Fanny said. Phoebe insisted that Fanny allow her to send a cab to pick her up for the meeting. But Fanny declared that her friend shouldn't worry about her.

"Now Fanny, you must listen to me," Phoebe said. "I cannot allow you to travel to the Hippodrome alone. Mr Moody's meetings draw crowds beyond anything you can imagine. The crush of people fill the sidewalks and the streets. And of course the crowds draw the usual pickpockets and vendors trying to sell every kind of souvenir, none of them approved by Mr Moody or Mr Sankey. You would most surely be crushed and lost in the crowds, Fanny. Mr Moody's work with the YMCA to reach the boys of the slums in Chicago has made him famous here, and his revival meetings in England drew thousands upon thousands to hear him and Ira Sankey." Phoebe did not stop for breath. "I know that the meetings in the great Brooklyn Rink were packed out with 7,000 inside and as many outside. People lined the streets at 7 a.m. for the opening of the building at 9 a.m." she said. "After he spoke the people, including the visiting ministers, were like an army ready to march out for the Lord. Young people left the meeting marching arm in arm singing "Hold the Fort, for I am Coming." Phoebe bent down to touch Fanny's hands busy knitting a gift for someone as they talked. "It is happening here in New York too, Fanny. Like a mighty storm, revival is awakening people through these men of God. You cannot possibly go without an escort but my dear, we will go together with a few of my friends and I shall pick you up at that tenement you insist on staying at, in plenty of time for us all to be seated."

Fanny sighed and went on knitting. Phoebe, satisfied that the matter was settled, sat down. "You are right," Fanny agreed. "I think I would be unwise to go alone, and I do so much want to hear Mr Sankey. I have heard that he has a voice of power and sweetness. Van told me that if he had not joined Mr Moody, Ira Sankey might have become one of the world's finest opera singers," Fanny said. "Mr Moody, cannot sing very well at all. He is called by some a backwoodsman with little education. Apparently he speaks with a New England accent, and often not with the best of English grammar. But," she added quickly, "I've also heard that he is a powerful man of God, chosen for these times. Of that there is no doubt."

"Oh I wish you could have seen Moody in Chicago when I was there," Phoebe said. "How those boys at the YMCA listened to his every word! He never scolds them, seldom speaks of the usual do's and don'ts so many ministers spend their time listing, but he speaks the gospel with great power. He is a solidly built man, not short or tall, and though his hair is short, his beard is quite gigantic." Phoebe laughed and Fanny chuckled at her description. "He is no musician as you said, Fanny, but Mr Sankey certainly makes up for that with his skills. "Sankey is a tall man, every bit a fine gentleman. His mustachios are the grandest mutton-chop whiskers, and I must say he dresses well." Fanny chuckled. If anyone knew about dressing well, it was Phoebe Knapp who loved fashionable things and often described them to Fanny in spite of Fanny's plain tastes.

"But what about his voice?" Fanny asked.

"Ah!" Phoebe continued. "Sankey sings with a fine baritone voice and with such feeling that I believe I have never heard the like before. Mr Moody says that for those who are not moved by preaching, the singing of the gospel will oftentimes reach hearts."

Fanny stopped her knitting as a thought came to her mind. "Phoebe, I've been thinking of all the thousands of people who now live in Manhattan. When I was a girl great numbers of Germans and Irish were coming. I've heard that 800,000 people live in New York City.

It's like a great mission field on our doorstep. I know God has sent Mr Moody and Mr Sankey to do a great work here, and I can't wait to meet them."

"And I shall see to it that you do," Phoebe promised.

When Fanny met them, they were as glad to meet her as she was eager to know them. "Ah, Miss Crosby," Mr Moody said in his New England accent, "at last, we have found you. Mr Sankey has sung your beloved song 'Safe in the Arms of Jesus' many times. And how it has touched hearts when we speak of death and resurrection, and that the child of God has nothing to fear."

"And I must tell you," Mr Sankey said, "that while we were in England your beautiful song 'Pass Me Not, O Gentle Savior' was so popular that it was sung every day at Her Majesty's Theatre in Pall Mall. It has already been translated into several languages. It is a joy to meet the Fanny Crosby behind so many well-loved gospel songs."

Not only were Moody and Sankey strong admirers of Fanny's hymns and using them often, but they wanted her to write new songs for them. Fanny could not have been happier when Ira Sankey asked for more and more of her songs to fill each new edition of *The Gospel Hymns and Sacred Songs* hymnal they used at meetings. Fanny gladly supplied them.

Fanny was at the office at Biglow and Main several days a week to work on the hymns she wrote for both the Sunday Schools and the evangelists. One of her remarkable gifts was that she could dictate two different poems to two secretaries at the same time without mixing them up. "Fanny, I don't know how you do it," one of her fellow workers said, one day. "Though I do know that your memory is a gift from God, I am still astounded by it."

Fanny smiled, "I know that you have your own gift from God as each of us does. For me there is only the little library in my mind that God has given me to use," she said.

"And your heart, Fanny. For that is where God's gift to you surely begins."

Fanny nodded. "If only our songs will take Jesus love into some empty heart, I will thank him forever for my small part in it."

Mail had come to the office for Fanny, as it often did these days. The secretary read her the letter that had just come inviting Fanny to speak for a missionary organization. "That will be fine. I think helping a mission church like that with their anniversary celebration will be a joy," Fanny said.

There were others to hear, and when the secretary finished, Fanny knew her schedule for the weeks ahead. "I don't know where you get such energy," the secretary said, "but I'm glad you have it." What she didn't say was that Fanny seemed to have the vigor of someone much younger than she was. She took as many invitations as she could, though some of them meant traveling a good bit. On top of speaking which Fanny felt she should do, especially in New York's prisons, she still made time to help with the work among the poor, and the outreach to her neighbors in the tenements.

That evening Fanny sat having a last cup of tea in the small kitchen of her friend Mary from the old neighborhood. The heavy odors of Mary's cooking for tomorrow's meal wafted about them. The halls and stairways would be heavy with the blended smells of many meals. Fanny had grown so familiar with the odors peculiar to tenement life that she barely noticed them anymore. It was time to go. She held out the guitar she had played for all of them earlier and said, "Mary, why don't you keep my guitar tonight. I won't need it tomorrow and I know your boy John loves to try it."

"Miss Fanny, that boy thinks you most close to an angel he ever gonna get this side the Jordan River. I believes he jest might be learning to play thanks to you. I saw his eyes shining this evening when you was teaching him. I'll see he takes good care of it."

As Fanny left and climbed the steps to her attic apartment, she heard Mary singing, "More like Jesus would I be." It was a song Fanny had written some time ago, but one that made her whisper now, "Thank you, Lord for all the Marys who sing it and mean it." Fanny hummed the next verse as she climbed the last few steps to her door. Tonight like most nights when the noises of the day grew still and the tenement slept, Fanny would work on a new hymn.

At last she settled in her chair. Fanny prayed and asked the Lord to bless her writing as she always did. And then she picked up the little book that waited for her on the table by her chair. Holding the small book in her hands she chuckled. "Lord," she whispered, "it is funny isn't it, that I love holding this little book in my hands when I need a song, or even when I'm asked to speak anywhere, or sing? I remember holding on to it back at the Institute, and I can't even see it at all, and it isn't a Braille book. It just feels good in my hands." She smiled as her fingers smoothed the well-worn covers of the little book, sometimes she used other small books if they were the right size. It didn't seem to matter what kind of book it might be. "Somehow I think it helps me remember every word and line I need to recall." How it helped was a mystery, but to hold a small book in her hands while she worked or recited was a life-long habit for Fanny. It certainly had helped her when Philip Phillips gave her a second list of forty more titles for songs that he needed Fanny to write. This time as before she wrote all forty in her mind, and dictated all forty at one time, each a finished song. Many times she would need to edit, but often the best hymns came complete and needed no editing.

Fanny was writing enough poems that Ira Sankey put some of them into the office safe for future use. Years later when Fanny was asked to say a word at a summer retreat she remembered a poem called "Someday" that she'd written and recited it. The audience wept. Sankey was excited and asked where Fanny had gotten the poem. "I wrote it for Biglow and Main, and I believe it has been in their safe waiting for music ever since. Sankey had a friend write the music and Fanny's hymn, "Saved by Grace" was sung by Christians everywhere. It was what one writer called Fanny's "Heart's Song." Though she was blind and had never seen, she had written:

> And I shall see Him face to face,
> And tell the story—Saved by Grace.

Fanny was writing for a long list of fine musicians and singers as well as for Sankey, and one of them was her old friend, Vet Main's son, Hugh Main. She loved Hugh's music and gladly wrote for him, including a love song, one of the popular secular songs that she sometimes agreed to write. Her pay remained the same. She still lived among the poor and chose to give away everything she did not need for Fanny had learned that God always supplied when she truly needed something. Like the day she had no money for bread or rent. After praying and asking God about her need she busied herself with household chores. Very soon there was a knock on the door. A visitor had come just to see Fanny and thank her for a hymn that meant so much to his family. When the man left he shook her hand leaving in it a small gift. It was the exact amount that Fanny had prayed about!

She was now middle-aged and busier than she had ever been, but never too busy for Anna and other friends from her days at the Institute. When she learned of losses or illness, or of joyful events like births and weddings her heart responded with poems for them. Thankfully, letters from friends and home came often. Her sisters were both married now, and her mother lived with her brother's family. It was family tradition that Fanny would write poems for the family's special events. Each year she wrote a poem for her mother's birthday, a mother who seemed to grow dearer to Fanny every year. On visits home Fanny delighted in the old familiar walks that brought back her childhood memories. Life was so busy now, but she always returned to her work with new energy, and could hardly wait to be back at the office of old Biglow and Main.

Fanny's songs were known and sung by Christians everywhere, thanks in part to Moody and Sankey. Often visitors to New York came to see her just to thank her and tell her how one of her songs had changed their lives. Fanny smiled as she thought of how often Mary and some of her other neighbors used to say "Ain't never thought fancy dressed folks be climbing these old tenement stairs to see you, Miss Fanny, but they sure does."

Fanny had always welcomed visitors, but these days she had become a visitor herself, a regular one at New York City's Home Missions. The rescue work of the missions was set in some of the worst parts of the city. She loved sharing the good news of Christ's love and pardon not just with her song writing, but face to face with those who needed to hear. She chuckled, "Blind I may be, but I've two good hands and two good feet to use as well as my mind," she thought.

Missions

The little old blind lady was a familiar sight in the Bowery, a New York neighborhood known as one of the worst slum areas of the city. Had Fanny not been blind she would have seen the beggars who'd lost arms or legs or both in the Civil War begging on every corner. She would have seen the drunks stumbling to and from the countless taverns, the raggedly dressed barefoot children, the vendors selling corn cobs, and raw oysters, and doorway after doorway leading to the city's vilest places. Fanny didn't see any of this, but she knew it was all there; she could hear the curses, the rude laughter, the fighting, all the sounds of misery. And she knew the way to the rescue missions where Christian workers held out hope and help to the most desperate of the city. Fanny went each week to help.

Since she could do her writing at night and some mornings at the office, she was free to do missions work in-between. She was headed today to the Bowery Mission church where she often went to help Pastor Rulifson and his wife. Sometimes the pastor asked her to talk to the men, but most often Fanny simply sat with them and listened and prayed. This evening she slipped into a chair well before the service. Someone soon came and sat down in the chair in front of her. Fanny knew from the sound of his steps, his hesitation, the odors of the street that clung to his clothes, that he was a visitor to the mission. It was quiet around them, and as they sat there Fanny felt moved to speak to him.

"Are you fond of music?" she asked him.

"Yes," he answered.

Fanny made her way to a chair next to the man, and sat down. For awhile she talked about music, and soon the conversation turned to things the man was interested in. When Fanny asked him if he knew what the sweetest words in the English language were he said "No, tell me."

"They are mother, home, and heaven," Fanny said.

The man was still for a moment and then he said, "My mother was a Christian." He said no more as the service began at that moment. The sermon that night was, "A Mother's Influence!" Only God could have planned this, Fanny knew.

Pastor Rulifson had finished and asked if anyone wanted to come forward for prayer. Fanny gently asked "Will you go?"

In the quiet of the moment, her new friend answered, "Will you go with me?"

"Yes, I will go with you," she said and taking his arm walked with him to the front where Pastor Rulifson waited for the young man Fanny was bringing, one who was weeping and ready to give his life to the Lord.

It was always Fanny's way to reach out to the needy, to draw them back to the Lord with kindness and the word of God. Whenever she was asked to speak to mission workers, she urged them not to condemn or point out a person's sin, "they know that already," she said. "Tell them that no one is too far down for the love of Jesus to reach them. I grieve to think how many people who come through our church doors slip away without a kind word of welcome," she said. One of the things she loved about Mr Moody's preaching was that unlike so many who preached hell-fire and damnation, he preached the power of Jesus Christ to save, the strong love of God for the lost.

Fanny meant for her songs to reach the lost with God's love and was glad they were widely sung at mission churches and revival meetings. Songs like "Rescue the Perishing," "Though Your Sins be like Scarlet they shall be White as Snow," "Only a Step to Jesus," and others that held out God's words of hope and rescue and love did bring many a lost and needy person to Jesus. When Phoebe and some of Fanny's friends insisted that Fanny should ask to be paid more for her hymns, Fanny refused. "God has given me a wonderful work to do," she said, "… that has brought me untold blessing and great joy. When I hear of some wandering soul being brought back home through one of my hymns my heart thrills with joy, and thanks to God for giving me a share in the work."

Fanny was in her sixties now, and busier than ever. Another mission she loved to visit was the work of Jerry McCauley. His had been one of the first home missions, the Water Street Mission near the East River. In his youth Jerry McCauley's life had been full of crime and drunkenness. Because of this he landed in the notorious prison, Sing Sing. Though wrongfully accused this time, he spent five years in a windowless, prison cell, and it was there that another prisoner led him to Christ. Since then thousands of men had passed through the McCauley Mission's doors. He and his wife had now opened a new outreach, the Cremorne-McAuley Mission, a three-story building with a chapel, a kitchen, and living space where those who came could be clothed and fed. Fanny visited often. The mission's rule was, "We hit our men with beefsteaks before we hit them with the gospel," and that was just fine with Fanny. The men who came to the mission were never scolded or even asked about their past lives. Over the years thousands of men who came to the mission found new life in Christ. When McCauley died, Fanny joined the hundreds who mourned the death of the thief who had become God's servant.

Fanny also went to the mission for fallen women, Mrs E. M. Whittemore's Door of Hope. Mrs Whittemore and her husband had stopped one night on their way to the theater to visit the McCauley mission. They'd stayed and that night given their lives to Jesus, and then to full time Home Missions. At Door of Hope Fanny often addressed the women when the Whittemores asked, but most of the time she simply sat among them, to talk with them and to listen to them. It was bad enough for men who were down and out, but in the society of the day women were judged far more severely and found little sympathy.

Fanny was a good listener, though often the women's stories were hard to bear. Like the men, many of the women felt that nobody cared for them and nothing could make a difference. "It's true, Miss Fanny, I ain't got no friends," a woman muttered. Her life on the streets had left the woman stripped of home and health and she'd come to the mission ready to give up. As she began to weep, Fanny put her arms around the woman and told her that she cared, and that there was another who cared, One who could make all the difference, the Lord Jesus! His love and pardon was waiting for her right now. When they walked together to the front of the church to kneel in prayer, it was Fanny's hymn "Only a Step to Jesus" that the pianist played.

Like small dots of light, Home Missions reached out to the thousands of poor and needy in New York's darkest streets and tenements. But even beyond the decaying neighborhoods to better ones, Fanny knew serious drunkenness was everywhere, crushing lives and ruining families. It gripped its victims until they could no longer break free. Alcohol was cheap and available even in the worst of slums. Fanny was often asked to speak at the Women's Christian Temperance

Union, that urged people to sign a pledge to abstain from alcohol. Fanny also wrote poems telling the sad stories of lives ruined by alcohol—poems and songs that moved many hearts to help the cause, and these were published by the Business-Men's Organization who pushed for moderation in drinking rather than no alcohol. Fanny said, "Whichever pledge will work is good, whether it's a pledge to drink only a small amount and never at work, or the pledge never to drink hard liquor, or a pledge not to drink at all." In the tenements Fanny had known the sadness and loss of too many lives, and their stories moved her own heart.

This morning at the office an invitation was waiting, and as the secretary read it Fanny clapped her hands for joy. Fanny had never been able to keep still when she was happy. The letter was from the YMCA's Railroad Branch, asking her to come and speak to the men at one of the new homes. Fanny called them her "Railroad Boys," and though she loved sharing at all the YMCA's work with young men, she especially loved those who worked as conductors on the trains and trolleys[1]. The YMCA provided safe places for these young men to live, have their meals, recreation, and meeting places for Sunday worship. "You know how often I ride the trolleys, and now the trains, and over the years I've come to know many of these young men," she explained. "What a joy it is to me to speak to them."

---

[1] A method of transport from the early to mid 20th Century, referred to as a tram in the United Kingdom.

And of course, she would have a poem just for them. Sometimes she simply told them how she'd come to write a song, one that might touch their hearts as well.

The next letter was from Phoebe. There was no one quite like her dear friend, Phoebe, who like a general in command of an army, loved to organize and plan, even what she thought was best for Fanny. "I know she is anxiously waiting to see how I will do traveling to Ocean Grove by myself next week." Fanny had refused all offers of an escort. "I will do just fine on the train, and I shall greet her on her own doorstep, or rather tent step," Fanny laughed. Phoebe was expecting her for a vacation at the Christian retreat center where everyone stayed in tents, even the fashionable Mrs Phoebe Knapp.

The secretary sounded a little wistful as he said. "I'd sure like to spend time there one of these days."

"I really can hardly wait," Fanny admitted. "I do love the beach, the sound of the ocean waves, and the wonderful meetings! People sing at the retreats as they do nowhere else! I will come back and still hear it in my memory."

"Yes," he agreed. "If anyone can play music in her mind, it is you, Miss Crosby."

Thousands upon Thousands

Vacation time was over, and Fanny felt as eager as she had ten years ago to be back at the work she loved. Phoebe had decided they should visit Northfield first, and today Fanny had visitors. There were too few seats in the small room where Fanny was staying, but the young people visiting her from Mr Moody's school at Northfield were right at home sitting on the floor. "Aunt Fanny, please tell us how you write, what method you use," one of the students pleaded.

Fanny who had often been at the Northfield campus, loved having the students visit her. Most of them called her Aunt Fanny, and like a fond aunt she welcomed them and their many questions. "Well," she said, "I know you will want to know first something about the thing you call 'mood.'"

"It's true that there are times when I simply cannot write. If any of you have had a dreadful toothache, or some other hard pain, you know that the thought of writing a poem or song has no chance at all," she said, and smiled, as someone agreed loudly. "But, if a song is needed right away, as often is the case, there are two things I do to get into what you might call the right mood to write. First, I need to be alone, somewhere quiet if possible, and then I need to pray for help to write that hymn. Praying before I write any song is something I try always to do. A song may come from something as simple as a cloudy day and a friend telling you that a single small ray of sun is breaking through. You may know the song 'Only a word for Jesus'." Several voices said that they knew that one. "Well, that came from that very kind of day."

"And," Fanny added, "You young people know how many times the joy inside us just overflows. I have heard some of you sing 'Praise Him, Praise Him' and I could feel the joy that filled the air." Her voice grew softer as she said, "And all of us know too those times when the heart is so full of deep need it grows so heavy we feel we cannot carry it alone. Such a time for me led to the hymn 'Lord Hold My Hand'." She sang a few lines and others soon joined in the well-known chorus.

"That was lovely, my dears," Fanny said. "Now I do need to remind you not all songs come by themselves like that, but more often I am given a topic by one of the composers. I like to take my assignments home in my mind so that I may write at night when it is quiet. It's the time I like best to write." Fanny paused, and then smiled as if a happy thought had just come to her. "Dear hearts," she said, "I told you that I pray for help to write each hymn, but I also ask God to use them to bring others to himself. Whenever I hear that someone has come to the Lord through a hymn I feel such joy to think God is using songs to reach lost hearts. So, there you have my method. Of course I do think of the meter," she added, "and I always finish a song before I dictate it to a friend. Many times I will want to change something when I hear it read back. I do like to write more than one poem so that my publisher may choose what he thinks best."

Someone asked a question about the musical setting for her hymns, and Fanny listened. "No," she said, "I don't write the music, though I have once. Usually someone will play a piece or even hum it for me, and then I will make a song to fit their music. Other times I write a poem for a subject given to me, and later on music is written for it. When I do that I will often fit it to a tune I know just to check its meter, but it too will have its own tune, eventually. During the war a song I wrote became so popular that after the war, we used the same tune as the setting for a new hymn. For me, what matters is that a hymn be a song anyone can easily remember and sing."

"Aunt Fanny," a young woman asked, "What is your definition of a hymn?"

"Thank you, for asking that," Fanny said. "My hope is that my answer will be one your heart tells you is so the very next time each of you sings a hymn. I believe," she said, "a hymn is the song of the heart addressed to God."

It was a young man who asked her the next question. "Aunt Fanny, you've written so many great hymns, but I wonder if you think sometimes how your life might have been if you had your eyesight?"

"A good question," Fanny said. "When I was just a child, I didn't know what seeing meant really, and blindness was natural to me. I think I might have thought most everyone was just like me. But when I grew a little older I learned there was a world out there and others could see what I could not. Back then blindness meant no education, no opportunities, and I longed for so much more. But God had a plan, a good one all along, and opened the door for education, musical training and here I am, dear ones, and would not exchange my life for anything." Fanny's face lit up, though she didn't see it, as she leaned forward and opened wide her arms as if to embrace them all. "Dear ones," she said, "I am shut away by my blindness from the distractions of the world, and it is not an affliction, but a gift from God."

"Well said," one of the students agreed, "and now Aunt Fanny, a song if you please!" Everyone agreed and begged Fanny for a song. Fanny's guitar was close by and soon she had them singing with her.

The following week a letter came for Fanny. Anna was coming to visit! It would only be for a day, but Fanny was so glad she went half an hour early to the great Grand Central Depot to meet Anna's train. In the crowd of noises and so many footsteps at the station Fanny could only wait until she heard Anna's voice saying, "Thank you, sir, my friend is blind too, and she should be here waiting for me."

Fanny called out, "Over here, Anna, I'm right here waiting." The kind gentleman who had assisted

Anna from the train soon escorted her straight to Fanny whose eager greeting loosed her bonnet to slip sideways.

"Anna, it's so good to hear your voice, your laughter. You sound just the way you did when we were students at the Institute. Oh, that deep, wonderful laugh of yours! Do you remember the times the two of us and Mary and sweet, timid Lucy carried out our midnight pantry raids, and how often you nearly gave us away because you could never keep from laughing so hard it made us all laugh until we could barely move."

Anna firmly tapped Fanny's arm. "Fanny, you know who was the ring leader back then, and from your letters I can tell that you still love a good joke," she said. She laughed and added, "Now, you must take us both to some little restaurant where we can lunch and you can answer my thousand and one questions."

Fanny linked her arm in Anna's and turned them both in the direction of the small restaurant she knew would be just right, a place she'd been to before. "You will love it," Fanny said. "They do have the best desserts."

"Fanny, speaking of desserts, I can tell just by your thin little arm that you are as tiny as ever. But sadly, you can surely tell by mine, that I am truly what my sister calls matronly."

Fanny chuckled. "Life in a small farm town with all that fresh milk and foods can only do anyone good. But really, Anna, I know I feel I could keep going for years to come, and my appetite is as large as ever."

Anna chuckled. Their chicken salads served with fresh buttery rolls and a delicate cream of potato soup came with a plate of fruit tarts and cheeses. They ate slowly as they talked. Fanny told Anna of the concert she and Van were soon to do for a family reunion of the Underhills, friends of Van's. "I hear their names in the newspapers often," Anna said, "supporting this charity or that. I know they are among New York's wealthiest families."

"Yes," Fanny said. "They dearly love Van and see him for the totally dedicated musician that he is. They have opened both their home and their hearts to him. I believe he satisfies their own passion for the classical arts. You know, Anna, though Van's music is wordless and highly difficult it is quite wonderful."

"I know too, Fanny, that you are quite capable of such music, but I love that you choose to write what so many need, songs that reach the heart," Anna said.

At last, even Fanny could eat no more, and Anna finished the remaining raspberry tart as the waiter refilled their tea. "Now, tell me all about your latest hymns, please, Fanny."

"I think one you will like is called 'Tell Me the Story of Jesus.'" Fanny sang it softly and Anna pressed Fanny's fingers against her face to feel the tears the song had brought.

"Thank you, dear heart," Fanny said. "I cannot sing them all for you here, but I will send you copies of 'Redeemed, How I love to proclaim It,' and 'Take the World, but give me Jesus,' and lastly one that is becoming quite popular, 'He Hideth My Soul in the Cleft of the Rock.' Their hours together went all too fast and soon the small chiming watch that Anna wore told her it was time to head back to the station.

The train was already waiting, and the conductor ready to assist Anna into it. Anna hugged Fanny tightly and promised, "Next time we will spend a weekend together and not just a day."

Fanny promised to write, and as the train filled and the conductor called a final "All Aboard" Fanny waited though she couldn't see Anna and Anna couldn't see her. In fact neither friend had ever seen the other's face. But that didn't stop Fanny from gently singing the lines "God be with you 'till we meet again".

Finally the train pulled away, its steam belching and iron wheels drowning out other sounds. Fanny wiped away a tear. This time, it was the kind of little tear that spilled from a heart full of good, happy memories. Oh how she had changed from the fearful, lonely, fifteen-year old girl she had been when she'd first arrived at the Institute! "You gave this blind child of yours everything I needed, Lord, and so much more," she thought. Only the week before when she'd prayed for five dollars she really needed, the same day a visitor had left that exact amount as a gift to her. The same night she'd written the hymn "All the Way My Savior Leads Me". The words came to her now and she hummed them as she walked.

The publishing office was close by and Fanny made her way there. Ira Sankey had just returned from Scotland. As the two of them talked, Sankey said, "Fanny, I promised to bring you a message from an old Scottish woman in Edinburgh. She wanted to thank me for writing 'Safe in the Arms of Jesus' and I told her it was Fanny Crosby who wrote it. 'Well,' she said, 'when you gang back to America, gie her my love, and tell her an auld Scots woman sends her blessing. The last hymn my daughter sang before she died, was that one.'"

"Thank you, for that message," Fanny said. "That song is dear to me too."

"And to countless others, Fanny," Ira said. "I have heard many stories like the old Scottish woman's. A young boy asked for that song as he lay dying, and I know it was the favorite of a little six-year old who sang it often before an illness took her life."

"Yes, it is a comfort to sing those words," Fanny agreed. "Pastor John tells me it is the one most comforting to many who lose a child." And Fanny knew what that was like.

"Miss Fanny Crosby I have come to steal you away!" It was Hugh Main, the son of her old childhood friend, Vet. Fanny loved the young man's humor and long ago had recognized his musical talent. He was one of the finest composers she knew. Hugh took her arm. "Yes, I shall battle this tyrant Mr Sankey, and rescue you at once if I must," he said.

Fanny smiled. "Well, I should not want any harm to come to Mr Sankey since I know him to be a good and godly man, young sir, but I believe he and I have finished our work for today. Am I right that you mean to share a new piece of music with me, and you know that I will be glad I listened?"

"You will be glad, I think," Hugh said, as he escorted her into the piano studio and led her to a nearby seat. "More than that, I have need of your best powers to form the words for my new love song. I have an idea for the title, 'O When Are You Coming to Me Again?'"

Before she could say a word, Hugh began to play and as Fanny listened, words came to her mind and line after lined formed, following the beautiful music as Hugh played. When he finished she recited the lines to him.

> *O when are you coming to me again?*
> *I'm waiting with heart so true,*
> *And wishfully chiding the long, long hours*
> *That keep me away from you.*
> *The cricket is chirping,*
> *Tis evening now,*
> *The time that we love so well;*
> *Then meet me alone, by the brook, mine own,*
> *The brook in the leafy dell.*

"I knew you were the one to write it, Fanny!" Hugh exclaimed. "You are the Queen of the Gospel Song, and from that same heart comes the purest and sweetest of love songs. I shall be in your debt forever, fair lady."

Fanny laughed and shook her head. "Hugh Main, I shall hold you to your promise, and expect a new birthday poem from you on every birthday left to me."

"And that you shall have," Hugh promised and chuckled. Each year since the publishing company had held a birthday celebration for Fanny, Hugh had sent her a humorous poem. He was fond of Fanny, and he made sure that every one of his birthday poems made her laugh. One of his birthday poems would read:

> *O Fanny, you're the worstest one,*
> *As ever yet I've knew,*
> *You ask for things inopportune,*
> *You du, you know you du!*
>
> *It's every year along in March,*
> *When tree toads 'gin to roam,*
> *You set me wilder than a hawk*
> *A howlin' for a pome.*

Fanny always kept the birthday poems Hugh sent her in her scrapbook right alongside cherished keepsakes. Hugh's were always among her favorites. Hugh's latest poem would be pasted in close by a clipping about "The performance of Mr Van Alstyne and Miss Fanny Crosby at a family reunion given by the Underhills at their home in Yonkers, New York."

The evening affair at the Underhills' family reunion had been a great success for both Fanny and Van. Fanny dressed in a fine gown, compliments of Mrs Underhill, had recited a long poem she'd written for the family, and she and Van had played beautiful pieces of classical music. Fanny performed on the harp, and Van at the piano. Van was a masterful pianist and Fanny could hear how the audience appreciated him.

The evening entertainment ended with thunderous applause. When Van saw her out to the waiting cab, he held her close. "Fanny, you were wonderful," he said. "Will you come to the Underhills' vacation home. I'll spend next week there before my fall schedule begins. They would love to have you visit, as I would, my dear."

"Oh, how I wish I could, Van, but I'm already booked to speak in two places next week before I go to Phoebe's vacation home and then to see my family at Bridgeport. After that I am truly busy. But I will think of you, Van, and pray you have a good rest, my dear. Please take care of yourself." Fanny allowed herself to be helped into the cab.

"I will write," Van called out as the cab pulled away.

Fanny sighed. "Watch over him, dear Lord," she prayed as the cab moved off. Then Fanny began to hum a tune. Every summer and Christmas her own family came together, and Fanny loved the reunions. Her sisters, Carrie and Julia and Fanny, would have their own little time together. Fanny hummed a bit more. She was trying to come up with a new birthday song for her Mother. Even though she had died a few years before Fanny still wrote those songs in memory of her. "Yes," she whispered, "that will be my new song for our mother. My sisters and I will sing this song when it is ready. The nieces and nephews will fill the house with hugs and endless games and I will write poems for them all.

Family reunions at Bridgeport were precious times. Fanny could hardly wait!

Four-Nine-Four, Boys!

Fanny had relocated again to Brooklyn! Hugh and young Allan Sankey had helped her move into the new room on Lafayette Avenue, and then taken her to dinner. As the two were finally leaving, Hugh teased her. "You know, Fanny old thing, Mrs Phoebe Knapp will never forgive us for letting you move into another poor neighborhood."

Fanny chuckled. "Then," she said, "I shall just have to tell her the choice was all mine, and you two boys could do nothing to change my mind. Besides, this place is closer to where two of my dear friends live. I can still visit my old neighbors, especially those in the tenements, and hope soon to be of some use here." Hugh laughed and bid her goodbye.

Fanny didn't hear him say to Allan as they left the building, "She does love the poor among us. I know she keeps not a cent more for herself than her needs demand, and I've known her to give away even some of that. She simply does the things Jesus told us to do."

Allan nodded. "Not long ago I heard my father and Mr Moody talking about how many people had come to the Lord because one of her gospel songs touched their hearts. They use her songs at every meeting. It is the gospel in songs. At last count we believe she has written 8,000 hymns."

"Yes," Hugh added, "and she has no plans to stop until the Lord says 'It's time!'" Allan smiled thinking of the little blind lady, who had just written a hymn for him called "Never Give Up."

Settled in her small, familiar rocking chair in her new room Fanny took up her knitting. She was finishing a new set of washcloths, the kind Van liked. Now that she lived in Brooklyn, and since Van's rooms with the Underhills were also in Brooklyn, it would be even easier for them to visit when their busy schedules allowed. And busy they were!

Biglow and Main, her publishers, needed two to three hymns a week, besides those Allan Sankey and Hugh and others asked her for. Thankfully, requests for her songs didn't seem to stop. She had written nearly 1,000 hymns for dear old Sweney, and Kirkpatrick, two fine composers, and quite a few others. A bit of wind rattled the window and Fanny listened a moment. Here she was in a snug room just right for her needs, but how many poor people, too many of them children, were out in the streets or in some wretched place this very night? The Bowery Mission, the Door of Hope, the Water Street mission, and the Cremorne Missions would be full tonight. The voices and stories of the down and out, drunkards, addicts, others she'd worked with at the rescue missions came often to her mind, and often to her prayers now. She finished the square of knitting and tucked it into the basket on the table beside her. As she did, her fingers felt the stack of letters she'd brought home from the office.

Most of them were asking her to speak in churches, at temperance meetings, Sunday School events, and one of her favorite groups, the Railroad Branch of the YMCA. She rarely turned anyone down if she could help it, and especially not her "Railroad Boys." The Railroad Branch of the YMCA had made her an official member of their group. "Busy, yes, Lord," she whispered, "but so thankful to you for every bit of it."

When a knock at her door and a familiar voice called "Fanny it's me, Ira and the missus come to see how you are settled in," Fanny smiled broadly and hurried to let them in. Her friends were family, and these two among the closest. "We shan't stay but a few minutes. We come bearing gifts," Ira said. "A fine new pillow to display, embroidered by none other than the famous Mrs Sankey, and a new shawl to keep you warm this winter."

Fanny made tea, and as they visited Ira told her the latest stories he had heard about her songs, one of them about a little blind Korean girl. "They call her little Miss Fanny Crosby," Ira said. "She is no more than six years old and can sing half-a dozen of your songs, Fanny, her favorite being 'Safe in the Arms of Jesus'." Fanny's heart warmed as she imagined the little Korean girl singing the very song that was so special to her own heart.

"Yes," Mr Sankey said, "it does warm the heart to think of it. But just imagine, Fanny somewhere in Africa they are singing your songs too. Bishop Taylor has been a missionary there all his life, and tells us how his people love Miss Fanny's gospel songs in their own tongue."

"That reminds me," Mrs Sankey said, "of the story of the British soldiers in the Transvaal during the South African War. They carried Ira's small pocket hymnal with them. We have heard that when one group of soldiers on the way to the front met another group they had a certain code they used to greet each other. One group called out 'Four nine Four, boys,' and the others answered 'Six further on, boys; six further on!' The numbers were from the tiny hymnals the soldiers carried. Number 494 was 'God Be With You Till We Meet Again'. And six further on was number 500, your song, Fanny, 'Blessed Assurance, Jesus is Mine!'"

Fanny was thrilled to hear the stories, and the evening ended all too soon. After they left Fanny made ready for bed, her first night in her new room. As always she knelt to pray. This time she began, "It's me, dear God, your blind child, and my heart is too full for words." She began to hum the song she'd used many times with children, one they sang loud and clear, "Praise Him, Praise Him". It was late when Fanny finally went to bed.

In the weeks and months that came and went, Fanny had little time to spare. Winter came and her new shawl helped warm her thin shoulders when the cold crept into her room. Fanny was happy as always, but soon close to Christmas the news came that her beloved old friend Mr Moody had died. "I have never known a kinder, bigger-hearted man than Dwight L. Moody. His work was a miracle, and a constant inspiration through all my work." She told the young reporter questioning her after the funeral. "His influence was like light…"she said. It was the highest tribute one who had been blind all her life, could make.

Fanny was glad these days for the friends who insisted on walking the icy streets with her and seeing her to work. She went as often as she could to help at the missions and was glad for offers to see her safely there too, but lately, she had not felt like her old self. She was with Hugh going over some new music when she felt something sharp in her chest and suddenly knew no more. Fanny woke up in a hospital bed. One day later, her sisters Carrie and Julia were at her side, insisting that she had lived long enough by herself.

"Fanny dearest, you are eighty years old and you've just had a heart attack. The doctor says you must rest and be cared for," Carrie pleaded. "I won't take no for an answer, Fanny. You are coming home to Bridgeport with me, and let me spoil you as much as I please." At the determined look on Fanny's pale face, Carrie used her softest voice to beg. "Fanny, I need you too. Ever since my dear husband's death, it has been hard to live alone. You will be doing me a great kindness, and also Julia too who will be close by."

Fanny smiled weakly. "Though I dearly love you both, only with one condition, will I move to Bridgeport. I must come back to New York whenever I need to, and go wherever else I need to go."

It was agreed, and after sixty-five years of living in New York, Fanny went home to Bridgeport with Carrie and Julie. What Fanny did not know was that Ira Sankey had arranged with Carrie to pay both her rent and see that she had a weekly stipend.

To everyone's amazement Fanny recovered and was soon back speaking, working at missions, and writing hymns. When she was at home in Bridgeport, Fanny helped at a local mission and visited patients at the local hospital, especially new patients. As often as needed she traveled back to New York by herself.

July came and Fanny went to Mr Doane's summer home in Rhode Island to work with him on a new hymnal, "Songs of Devotion." When a telegram came for her to tell her that her dear Van had died of a stroke at the Underhill's home, Fanny covered her face and wept. She arranged for Van's burial in Maspeth, Queens where they had made their first home together. In memory of Van she wrote the words:

> *And though at times the things I ask*
> *In love are oft denied,*
> *I know He gives me what is best*
> *And I am satisfied.*

> *From Him my soul, in life or death,*
> *No power shall e'er divide;*
> *I read the promise in His word*
> *And I am satisfied.*

In the days following Van's death, she found comfort writing hymns. Then Fanny was traveling again! "Rest is for old people," she told Carrie, "I believe I would not live a year if my work were to be taken away from me." In Lynn, Massachusetts she spoke at the YMCA. Fanny told them the story of how she came to write "Rescue the Perishing" after she had led a young man at one of the missions to the Lord. In his new joy he had told her that now he could meet his mother in heaven when the time came, because he had found her God. The meeting was over when an older gentleman took Fanny's hand and said, "Miss Crosby, I was the boy who told you more than thirty-five years ago that I had wandered from my mother's God. That evening you spoke I found peace… and if we never meet again on earth, we will meet up yonder." He left and Fanny never knew his name, but her heart was full of thanks for his new life in the Lord.

Fanny was in Bridgeport when she learned that Ira Sankey was sick. Her close friend who had loved and sung her songs and worked with her on so many, was seriously ill, and now like Fanny, he had become totally blind. Fanny began making regular trips to visit her friend at his home in Brooklyn. From the library shelves in her mind she read the Bible to him, and urged him to sing with her hymns they had written together. When Fanny came, Sankey would call out, "I hear her voice, send her up, for I declare she cheers me greatly." Her visits he said, made him feel "as if an angel-hand of strength, had been held out to him."

On the last visit they were to have, Ira asked Fanny to meet him in heaven. "There," he said, "I'll take you by the hand and lead you along the golden street, up to the throne of God, and there we'll stand...and say to Him: 'And now we see Thee face to face, saved by Thy matchless, boundless grace!'" The words were from the song "Saved by Grace" that Fanny had written and meant with all her heart, as Ira did now. Fanny did not see her dear friend, but she was told that on the morning Ira Sankey died he was singing the first lines of her song "Saved by Grace" singing his faith just before he slipped into a comma. Fanny thought of dear Ira and whispered the lines:

> And I no more as now shall sing
> But, Oh, the joy when I shall wake
> Within the palace of the King!

Months later Fanny spoke in Buffalo, New York. Before she was to speak that evening, the soloist stood and sang "Saved by Grace," but as he came to the third stanza, Fanny suddenly stood up and began to sing with him. As they sang together, Fanny's voice grew stronger and sweeter and by the time the two finished, many in the audience wept.

Without a song of faith in her heart Fanny would not have known how to bear the death of so many she had known and loved over her long lifetime. A letter had come and as Carrie read it, Fanny wept. Phoebe Knapp, her dear friend, Phoebe had died. How many songs had they sung together? How dearly Phoebe had loved hymns. She would have said, "Don't weep, Fanny, sing for me." Through her sorrow the words of a hymn she'd written long ago, "Dark is the Night," came to her. Ira Sankey told her he had sung it the night of the Chicago Fire as he sat in a small rowboat on Lake Michigan with heat and threatening death all around as the city burned. "Carrie, will you sing with me 'Dark Is the Night'?" Fanny asked. Together they sang the words:

> Dark is the night, and cold the wind is blowing,
> Nearer and nearer comes the breakers' roar;
> Where shall I go, or whither fly for refuge?
> Hide me, my Father, till the storm is o'er.
>
> Dark is the night, but cheering is the promise;
> He will go with me o'er the troubled wave;
> Safe He will lead me through the pathless waters,
> Jesus, the mighty one, and strong to save.

Carrie put her arm around Fanny's shoulder. "We have hope in Jesus, Fanny, dear."

"Oh, Carrie, what would I do without you?" Fanny said. For six years Carrie and Fanny lived together, and then, Carrie, who had been her eyes, her companion, her secretary, her cherished little sister also died.

Fanny was to live now with her young niece, Florence and her husband Henry, whom Fanny cheerfully called "the Governor."

All's Well, Governor

"Here you are, Hugh," Fanny said handing him the secretary's copy of the hymn, "We're Traveling On," that she had just finished for Hugh. She continued to write hymns for Allan Sankey and Charles Gabriel as well as some for Hugh.

"Dear Lady," Hugh said as he finished singing and playing the last line, "it is exactly what I needed, and finer than I could have imagined."

"Well, young man," Fanny teased, "I'm pleased that you like it, and you will understand that traveling on is just what I'm off to do this very afternoon. I go back to Bridgeport where I'm expected to lecture at the Christian Union, and hope to do some visiting here and there."

Hugh took Fanny's hand in his and she could feel him bowing. "I your humble servant, will await your return, my Lady. But don't forget that there will be work waiting for you right here. I've other songs in mind for you. And should you forget, remember that your birthday is coming, and if you want another birthday poem you must return ready to work!"

Fanny laughed. Hugh's poems were always the ones that made her laugh. "Just you be ready with that poem," she commanded.

In Bridgeport, the conductor helped Fanny down from the train. He knew Miss Crosby well, and that a certain cabby would be waiting for her arrival. "Right on time," the conductor said. "Your cab is waiting, Miss Crosby." Fanny thanked him and gratefully took the arm of the cabby man whose cheerful voice greeted her. It was known to all the other drivers that he alone was her private, devoted cabby, ready to drive her every place she needed to go. He never even charged her for the work he did. Fanny was thankful for his kindness, "Dear man," she thought. "And thanks to the new phone at my niece's house, he knew just when I would arrive. It's so good to be back in Bridgeport among family and friends," Fanny thought to herself.

"Will you be needing a ride to the missions tomorrow?" the cabby asked.

"Now how did you know that I can't wait to begin visiting there, and the patients at Rectors, you are such a blessing to me," Fanny said.

"And you, Miss Crosby to me and the missus, and a heap of others," he replied.

Each time Fanny was at home in Bridgeport, visitors came in great numbers to the house, some to meet her, others for help of one kind or another, some just out of curiosity, and even some for her autograph. After one woman asked if Fanny would give her the small cross Fanny wore for a keepsake and left with it in her hand without even a thank you, Florence, her niece insisted on being present during such visits.

Fanny still wrote, lectured, and traveled to speak at events. At age ninety-one she traveled alone back to New York City to speak at a grand church event. She stepped from the automobile that had been sent to fetch her, a small, frail, old lady dressed in her old fashioned clothing, and at once someone cried out, "For pity's sake, get her a wheelchair!"

Fanny quickly squelched the idea in her strongest voice. "I need no rolling chair," she said. "I can stand on my own two feet. My strength is in the Lord." As she entered Carnegie Hall packed with five thousand people, a choir of two-thousand sang, "We're Traveling On." A few months later Fanny traveled again alone to New York to visit friends and speak at her beloved Bowery Mission. It was the last time she returned to New York City. During her many years in New York, Fanny found her way around the city, on trolleys, subways, and to the right addresses, always able to count on the help of kind passersby. The city had changed! This time Fanny found that she was ignored, and on one trolley ride was pushed and shoved and made to stand for sometime before a conductor noticed her blindness, and called out for someone to give her a seat.

Fanny fell ill with pneumonia that fall, recovered to the surprise of Florence and the Governor, as Fanny loved to call Florence's husband, but some actually thought she had passed away. Far from it, Fanny still spoke and even traveled at times though now with her niece Florence. She was ninety-three, but could still speak as she did at Cambridge, Massachusetts to two thousand people. Back in Bridgeport she wrote hymns and poems for people, knitted, and welcomed a steady stream of visitors. One special night Fanny's old friend George Stebbins came with blind singer Jenny Carpenter for a program at Fanny's church. As Mrs Carpenter sang "Saved By Grace" Fanny rose and taking her arm, sang with her. It was a moment for tears and joy.

The following day Fanny had a visitor from England! This time Florence left the two of them alone in the parlor. "Miss Crosby," the woman began after Fanny had shaken her hand, something she liked to do because she felt a handshake could tell her so much about a person. "I've waited almost two years for the chance to meet you and thank you," her visitor said.

Fanny motioned to the chair next to her own. "Please sit here by me," she said.

"Miss Crosby, it was near two years ago that my son, Will, took sick. Just a lad he was, but oh how he loved to sing in the church choir. Well we knew the end was coming, poor lad, and it's that very end I've come to tell you about. He called me to bring the hymnal to him, and weak as he was, Miss Crosby, he chose the song 'Safe in the Arms of Jesus' and began to sing it." The woman's voice trembled a bit as she went on. "When he came to the words, 'Hark the voice of angels' he dropped the book, his face lit up and he said, 'Ma, there are the angels. There are the fields of glory...,' and then he passed on to be with ...his Lord forevermore." Fanny turned to hold the woman close and rock her as she wept. Softly, Fanny finished the hymn with tears of her own running down her face.

There were other visitors that came to tell her their stories too. One business man also from England, told how drinking had taken hold of his life and was fast bringing him down when he'd heard the song "Pass Me Not O Gentle Savior" at a Moody and Sankey meeting, and it made him long not to be left behind. The next night he'd gone back and heard the same hymn, and this time he'd asked Jesus to come into his life. That had been forty years ago. From his pocket the visitor took a copy of her hymn and pressed it into Fanny's hand. "This is a copy of that hymn," he said, "and I carry it with me always."

Fanny was nearly ninety-four when she made her last big trip with Florence to speak in Longmeadow, Massachusetts. This time she spoke at an outdoor garden event. She felt so well that she spoke and sang until Florence wisely and gently brought the program to an end. Back home in Bridgeport, Fanny had a mild heart attack, and this time the doctor warned that she could not live many more months. Fanny was anything but sad. "When I have arrived at my eternal home, they will say, 'Come in, Fanny! Come in!' And meanwhile I have work to do!"

Fanny could not go and visit but she could pray, and she could still write hymns! Allan and Hugh were planning a new hymnal and needed Fanny's songs. Fanny stayed busy writing a dozen hymns for them. The Great War in Europe had begun, and one of the hymns Fanny wrote, though it was a war hymn, ended with a prayer for peace.

January cold had set in when news came that her dear old friend Doane was very ill. He was now confined to bed and unable to sit up for longer than a few minutes each day. Would Fanny write one last piece for him? Fanny did, not knowing that it would truly be her last hymn. Thinking of dear Doane's coming death, she wrote to encourage him:

> At evening time it shall be light,
> When fades the day of toil away,
> No shadows deep, no weary night,
> At evening time, it shall be light.

> At evening time it shall be light,
> Immortal love from realms above
> Is breathing now the promise bright,
> At evening time it shall be light.

Visitors came and went, some of them asking Fanny to pray for them, which she promised to do. Sometimes a visitor would still ask her the old question about how she felt about her blindness. Fanny smiled and always told them how blessed she was with her blindness. What she didn't say was something she had shared with D. L Moody once when she told him, "I am so glad… that the first face I see will be the face of the Lord Jesus."

Fanny usually worked late into the night, and slept late, and Florence was glad when her aunt chose to stay in bed one day and allow herself to be waited on and pampered a little. Each time Florence checked in on her, Fanny was happy and smiling, and insisted that she was truly comfortable. One of the family nearby had lost a small child to illness and Fanny had spent time thinking of them that day. By evening she had written a poem and asked her friend Eva, to write a letter for her to the family and include the poem that ended: "Love will hold me fast and true." They were the last words Fanny wrote.

Florence had gone to bed earlier and Henry, her husband went to say a last goodnight to Fanny. As he peeked in, Fanny heard his familiar footsteps and smiled. "All's right Governor," she said. A few hours later Fanny became ill. Before dawn the family called their doctor but in spite of all they could do, Fanny was gone.

Bridgeport had never had such a funeral as large as Fanny's. Crowds who came lined the streets to pass by her casket. In Fanny's right hand was the little flag she loved to pin to her dress. Hugh Main and Allan Sankey were among those who had loved Fanny and worked with her and stood now weeping. However, they knew that their beloved Fanny Crosby could now see her Lord and Savior, the one she had loved and served all her life.

Everyone at the funeral received a violet and each dropped their violet into the casket until Fanny slept under a cover of violets, her favorite flower. The choir sang the words of Fanny's hymn "Saved By Grace".

> *Some day the silver cord will break*
> *And I no more as now shall sing.*
> *But, O, the joy when I awake*
> *Within the palace of the King.*

The New York Times wrote that Fanny Crosby's hymns reached "into every country of the world where the Christian religion has reached." Those who knew Fanny could have added: tenements, rescue missions, cities, countryside. From all backgrounds people who hadn't yet met Fanny Crosby were singing her simple songs whose words were prayers they could sing.

Many years have passed since Fanny's day, music tastes have come and gone, but there are songs that remain, songs like "Saved By Grace" and others. These are as Fanny would say, "Messages of the heart to God."

For a full list of Trailblazers, please see our website: www.christianfocus.com
All Trailblazers are available as e-books

Author Notes

Fanny Crosby was born into a poor family and spent her life ministering to the poor and needy, the prisoner, and whoever would listen. Though she was blind from infancy, her ministry through songs reached countless numbers of people with the good news of Jesus.

Fanny Crosby's answer to those who asked her how she felt about being blind was simple. "I think you should know that I do not consider myself afflicted," she said. "I think of my blindness as a gift from God." Behind all of Fanny's songs, some say 9,000, was her love for the Lord Jesus and her trust in his Word. That song in her heart became thousands of songs to bless many. Though today's musical tastes have changed, the Fanny Crosby songs we do sing, like "Saved by Grace," still bless us today. As Fanny would say, they are messages of our hearts to God that all of us can sing.

Fanny Crosby's life story is a reminder to all God's children that yes, God does have a place in his world for each of his children. And yes, nothing is impossible to God who can take our smallest gift and multiply it. It does not matter what our problems are, when we ask God if he has any place for us in his world, he hears us, and we can trust his good plans. And when we give him all we have to give him, he is able to make it more than enough for our own joy and his.

Fanny Crosby:
Timeline

1820	Born March 24 in the village of Southeast, Pultnam County, NY; six weeks later a treatment for an eye infection left her permanently blind.
1820-1834	Crosby and family lived in several locations in New York State and in Connecticut.
1829	Invention of braille printing.
1830s	Invention of passenger rail travel, the telegraph, photography and farm reaper.
1835	Entered the New York Institution for the Blind, where she stayed as student and then teacher until 1858.
1840s	Invention of the rotary printing press, the sewing machine and turbine engines.
1841	Crosby's first published poem, in the *New York Herald* newspaper.
1844	Crosby published her first book, *A Blind Girl and Other Poems*.
1849	Cholera epidemic in New York City.
1850s	Invention of the ice-making machine, gas burner, steelmaking furnace, and rechargeable storage battery.
1851-1857	Crosby and collaborator George F. Root wrote at least 60 songs, and three cantatas, for the general public.

1853	Crosby's second book published, *Monterey and Other Poems*.
1858	Married fellow-teacher Alexander Van Alstyne on March 5; third book of poems published, *A Wreath of Columbia's Flowers*.
1859	Only child born, died a few weeks after the birth.
1860s	Invention of linoleum, ironclad warship, train sleeping-car, typewriter and underground railway.
1861-1865	The American Civil War, during which time Crosby wrote several pro-Union songs.
1864-1915	Crosby's fifty-year career of writing hymns and gospel songs.
1870s	Invention of the telephone, microphone, phonograph and incandescent lamp.
1880s	Invention of the fountain pen, steam turbine, electric trolley car, phonograph records, pneumatic tire, motorcycle.
1890s	Invention of rayon, zip fastener, the submarine, color photography, the wireless.
1900s	Invention of the airplane, helicopter, safety razor, vacuum cleaner, cellophane.
1902	Husband Van died on July 18.
1915	Fanny died on February 12, just a few weeks short of her 95th birthday.

Thinking Further

1. Through Grandmother's Eyes

Fanny's grandmother helped her see the world around her. When Fanny began to realize her blindness was making a difference between her and sighted children, what encouraged her to be happy? Can you think of times that praying has encouraged you or someone you know? What does God say about prayer in Hebrews 11:6, 1 Thessalonians 5:17?

2. The Landlady's Gift

How did Fanny memorize the Bible? Why is learning God's Word so important? See John 14:23. Fanny couldn't answer her grandmother's question about meeting her in heaven. Why can people believe in God and still not be sure they are going to heaven?

3. I Shall put her on the Mantel

Have you ever had to make a difficult choice? How did you feel? Fanny had to choose between going on to school or going back home. New schools, classes, moving, all of them can bring us fears and sometimes tears. What helped Fanny? What things have helped you at times like that?

4. The Shape of her Head Will Tell

Mr Jones told Fanny that she needed to watch out for flattery and see her poetry as a gift from God. Are our talents just something we are naturally good at? 1 Corinthians 12 talks about God's gifts to us. What do verse 4 through 6 tell us?

5. The Blind Girl's Poem

Fanny loved a good joke and it sometimes got her in trouble. What does the Bible say about a cheerful heart in Proverbs 17:22, 15:13, 15:30? How did Fanny cheer Lucy whose terrible accident had left her disfigured? What did Fanny mean when she told Lucy the blind children would see her "With their hearts as I do?" Where does God look at a person? (see 1 Samuel 16:7).

6. Just Too Busy

What important question was Fanny too busy to think about? Fanny and Lucy didn't know for sure who can go to heaven. Who do you think can be sure of going to heaven? Why can someone be sure? In John 14:2-3 what does Jesus say to those who believe in him?

7. Bring Out Your Coffins

The cholera plague was a terrible sickness that left thousands dead. Afterward Fanny felt tired and empty. She still didn't know if she would go to heaven when she died. At the revival meetings the song "Here Lord, I give myself away" changed Fanny's heart and gave her peace at last. Can you explain what happened to Fanny at the revival?

8. A Love Song

Fanny's meeting with Mr Root leads to the start of her song writing career. Her meeting Van, a student at the school, leads to their marriage. Can we be sure that God is involved and cares about our future careers, even our future wife or husband? What does Psalm 139 say about God's doings in our lives?

9. A Deep Sorrow

When we or someone we know suffers the loss of a family member or friend there is grief. Fanny felt like she would never heal and it showed in her life. If you've ever felt that way you may remember how it touched everything around you. Can you think of things that do help us through grieving?

10. She Would Write Hymns!

How did Pastor Stryker help Fanny? Think of people who have helped you through a difficult time. Discuss Fanny's dream. Do you think God might use a dream to get someone's attention? Fanny is hired by Mr Bradbury and she is finally sure that writing hymns is God's will for her. What are some of God's promises about leading us? Look up Proverbs 16:3, Psalm 32:8.

11. Help me Speak to Them

"Rescue the Perishing" became one of Fanny's most loved songs . If Jesus Christ is the only Savior, the only way to heaven, why should we be telling the good news of Jesus to others? What did Jesus tell his followers to do in Matthew 28:19-20? Think of some of the things God has done for you.

12. Mr Moody and Mr Sankey

Fanny hoped her songs would take Jesus' love into empty hearts. Her songs were easy to sing and to remember and touched the hearts of many. Today organizations like Samaritan's Purse and Blythswood Care give out thousands of Christmas shoe-boxes to needy children all over the world. Each box contains gifts and a book about Jesus. In what way could you take the love of Jesus to empty hearts today?

13. Missions

Fanny taught that no one is too far down for the love of Jesus to reach them. What kinds of people might feel that Jesus could never love them? How big a sin will God forgive? (see Isaiah 1:18 and 1 John 1:9) Fanny was a good listener. Why is it important to listen to others?

14. Thousands Upon Thousands

One day a friend told Fanny of a tiny bit of sunlight shining through the clouds, and Fanny wrote the song "Only a word for Jesus." How might a word for Jesus be like a bit of sunshine for someone? Fanny said her blindness was a gift from God. Why do you think she said that? See Romans 8:38-39? How might the way Fanny felt about her blindness help someone?

15. Four-Nine-Four, Boys!

Why do you think the soldiers used the code in this chapter's title when they met fellow soldiers? Talk about the hymn "Dark is the Night:" why do you think Ira Sankey sang it during the great Chicago Fire? Why do you think Fanny asked Carrie to sing it with her when her friend Phobe died? What is our comfort when we believe in Jesus? See 1 Thessalonians 4:13-14.

16. All's Well, Governor

In this chapter how did God use Fanny's songs, "Safe in the Arms of Jesus" and "Pass me not, O Gentle Savior" to affect the life of a dying boy and an alcoholic man? How did God use Fanny Crosby's life to bring his love to many? If you were asked to write something on Fanny's gravestone what do you think you might write?

Being Blind Today:
Some thoughts from Hannah Harriman, a blind teenager

Christians are one of the most understanding groups of people when it comes to accepting blind people for the way they are. This is because we believe that God has a plan and purpose for everyone's life, no matter what their abilities are. But there are still some things you can do to help:

Don't be afraid to talk. Don't ask other people questions about me. Don't talk about me; talk to me. I want people to get to know me for me; I don't want to become someone's service project. It's embarrassing to have one of my parents helping me around. I'd rather be assisted by one of my peers. While I do appreciate people's assistance, I don't want that to be the only reason that they're with me. I want to get to know them, and I want them to get to know me. The same thing goes for the school setting. I try to encourage my peers to talk to me.

I encourage all types of questions: anything from "How did you lose your vision?" to "How do you have dreams?". No question is too offensive; it's more offensive to have people too embarrassed to talk to me.

Some Christians think that because Jesus healed a blind person that all blind people should be healed. I personally don't mind being blind. I'm used to it and I'm thankful God made me this way. He has a specific plan for my life. I don't think of myself as blind; there are many characteristics I give myself before the word "blind" crosses my mind: a good singer, an advocate, hardworking student, and above all, a Christian who lives to serve God.

Blindness doesn't make life challenging; it just requires minor adaptations of how to do things. The first thing is to have a positive outlook on life, despite the challenges. I have a few things that I do differently than my sighted peers so that it works for me. I use a cane and read Braille. By using a cane, I can know where I am going, but not have to rely on someone else to get me there. I memorize my route; I know how to navigate the high school I attend; I know how to get around church as well as numerous other places in the community. In the same way that a cane enables me to travel independently, Braille allows me to read for myself and not have to rely on others to read or transcribe for me. That doesn't go without saying that I don't ever need people to read things for me. On the contrary, that's needed more often than it should be. Menus in restaurants, street signs, and maps are just a few examples. However, with new technology that's coming out I can access things that previously have always been thought of as inaccessible to the bind. I'm sure that no one ever thought that blind people could use computers or even an iPhone or iPad, however over 4,000 blind and visually impaired do use iPhones.

Hannah Harriman

Hannah reminds us all that advocacy is important both for the blind and for the deaf community. Hannah has been blind from birth and is also profoundly deaf in one ear. Her active engagement in public speaking and advocacy for these communities has given her a dream for the future in politics as well as in developing her gifts in music.

My hope is that Hannah's thoughts on her own blindness will promote some discussions as you think about Fanny Crosby and the Hannahs of today.

Lucille Travis

CHRISTIAN FOCUS PUBLICATIONS

Christian Focus | Christian Heritage | CF4K | Mentor

Christian Focus Publications publishes books for adults and children under its four main imprints: Christian Focus, CF4K, Mentor and Christian Heritage. Our books reflect our conviction that God's Word is reliable and Jesus is the way to know him, and live for ever with him.

Our children's publication list includes a Sunday School curriculum that covers pre-school to early teens, and puzzle and activity books. We also publish personal and family devotional titles, biographies and inspirational stories that children will love.

If you are looking for quality Bible teaching for children then we have an excellent range of Bible stories and age-specific theological books.

From pre-school board books to teenage apologetics, we have it covered!

Find us at our web page:
www.christianfocus.com

CF4•K
*Because you're never
too young to know Jesus*